"A FIELD MANUAL;
BECAUSE IT NEEDS TO BE TAKEN INTO THE FIELD"

THE FIELD MANUAL FOR THE CHURCH DRUMMER

"*The Field Manual for the Church Drummer* is a practical and honest account of how to love what you do and how to serve your church within that. As a drummer, disciple, and artist, AJ explores ideas that will hopefully help you to not only give your best, but also stay sane and rooted. It's been a pleasure to work with AJ over many years as part of our team and this book comes out of a heart to learn, to serve, and to encourage others."
Colse Leung, Worship Pastor (Woodlands Church)

Praise him with the clash of cymbals, praise him with resounding cymbals. (PSALM 150:5)

FOREWORD

Firstly, I would like to say a big thank you for even just looking at this book! Worshipping through music is such a huge component of what we do in Church that it inevitably carries a great deal of weight and importance. Hopefully this book captures that and is a helpful aid to not just the drummers, but all the musicians and leaders in your Church.

This book was designed with one goal in mind:
To be a tool that equips and guides the drummers serving throughout the Church.

If you're a drummer then grab a copy of this book (preferably don't steal one) and jump right in! If you're a worship leader then get a copy for your drummer! If you're a Pastor then get a copy to give to both your drummer AND worship leader. If you are friends with a drummer in your church, you now have a great Christmas present idea.

My hope with this product is that churches around the country will see an increase in their musical worship, therefore having more ways of connecting deeper with the God who is longing to meet with them.
I really believe that the first step towards this is to equip the drummers.

Enjoy, and happy drumming!
God Bless.

AJ ROUSELL

CONTENTS

CHAPTER 1: AN INTRODUCTION TO THE FIELD MANUAL
- INTRODUCTION 06
- WHY? 07
- WHO? 07
- HOW? 08
- THE AUTHOR 09
- APPRECIATIONS 10

CHAPTER 2: UNDERSTANDING THE IMPORTANCE
- UNDERSTANDING THE IMPORTANCE 14
- WHERE WORSHIP & DRUMS MEET 16
- THE STARTING POINT 18

CHAPTER 3: GIVING YOUR BEST
- GIVING YOUR BEST 22
- GENERAL ETIQUETTE 23
- GETTING THE BEST FROM YOUR EQUIPMENT 27
- TUNING GUIDE 31
- SOUNDCHECK ETIQUETTE 34

CHAPTER 4: PRE-SERVICE & THE BAND
- PRE-SERVICE & THE BAND 40
- READ THE SOUNDCHECK & PRACTICE 41
- THE FOUR BASS PLAYERS 46
- TEMPERAMENTAL TEMPO 49

CHAPTER 5: IN THE FIELD
- IN THE FIELD 60
- PLAYING IN CHURCH 101 61
- THE ART OF DYNAMIC PLAYING 64
- USING RATES OF NOTES (SUBDIVISIONS) 69
- 6 ESSENTIAL DRUM GROOVES 71
- CHANGING THE FEEL, NOT THE GROOVE 76
- THE EXAMPLE 80
- WHEN STUFF GOES WRONG 82
- READY, SET, WORSHIP! 86

CHAPTER 6: THE INVITATION
- THE INVITATION 94
- THE INITIAL CONTACT 95
- SETTING OFF 96
- WHAT TO KEEP IN YOUR BOOT 97
- WHAT TO KEEP IN YOUR STICK BAG 98
- PRE-SERVICE INTEL 100

CHAPTER 7: THE INTIMATE CHURCH

- THE INTIMATE CHURCH 104
- THE DIFFERENCE IN EQUIPMENT 105
- DRUMMERS HATE/ARE UNABLE TO PLAY QUIETLY 107
- THE DRUM KIT ALTERNATIVES 111
- THE IMPACT OF PERCUSSION 113
- MINIMAL MICROPHONES 114
- HYMNS VS CONTEMPORARY WORSHIP 115

CHAPTER 8: THE HYBRID DRUMMER

- THE HYBRID DRUMMER 122
- ELECTRONIC DRUM KITS 123
- SAMPLE PADS & CHOOSING SOUNDS 126
- BACKING TRACKS 127
- CLICK PRACTICE 132
- DRUM TRIGGERS 135
- DRUM SCREENS 136

CHAPTER 9: THE TERMINOLOGY

- THE TERMINOLOGY 140
- POTENTIAL REQUESTS 141
- COMMON MIS-WORDINGS 146

CHAPTER 10: WHO NEEDS WHAT

- WHO NEEDS WHAT? 153
- WHAT A DRUMMER NEEDS FROM THEIR WORSHIP LEADER 154
- WHAT A WORSHIP LEADER NEEDS FROM THEIR DRUMMER 158
- WHAT A BASSIST NEEDS FROM THEIR DRUMMER 162

CHAPTER 11: REMOVING 'L' PLATES

- REMOVING L PLATES 167
- PLAYING WITH BEGINNER MUSICIANS 167
- RAISING UP NEW MUSICIANS 170

CHAPTER 12: THE DRUMMER'S WORSHIP

- THE DRUMMERS WORSHIP 177
- BEING IN A WORSHIP BAND, AND BEING A WORSHIPER 179
- IT SHOULDN'T MATTER WHERE YOU ARE IN THE ROOM 180
- THE STORY BEHIND CHAPTER 3 184
- WORSHIPPING THROUGH OUR INSTRUMENT 186
- WORSHIPPING THROUGH OUR CHARACTER 188
- FINAL WORD 190

"TO PROVIDE **A TOOL** THAT BETTER EQUIPS THE DRUMMERS THAT ARE SERVING THROUGHOUT THE CHURCH"

ONE
INTRO

THE FIELD
MANUAL

1

AN INTRODUCTION TO THE FIELD MANUAL
WHY, WHO AND HOW?

Firstly, thank you for even picking this book up. That in itself means so much. This book was written with a number of aspects in mind and was designed to serve in a variety of ways. My sincere hope is that it is helpful, beneficial, and insightful for whoever is reading it.

The worship of a church is such a special component that it is important to value and evolve. Some churches are incredibly fortunate with the number of musicians they have and the calibre of their playing. Some churches are near the other end of the spectrum and have difficulty finding the musicians they crave, resulting in either brand new musicians stepping up or even someone learning an instrument to serve their church.

All churches are different and all churches are unique, and this book was written to serve them all. Before we jump into the content, here is a brief overview of WHY the book was written, WHO the book was written for and HOW the book works:

WHY?

This book was written with one goal in mind;
To provide a tool that better equips the Drummers that are serving throughout the Church.

Worship is a unique and crucial element to the life of the church, so helping musicians to better themselves and their ability to serve in this form has always been a great passion of mine. Drummers are crucial to the overall sound of a band, so providing a tool that can help them push their playing, their awareness, and their own worship was the concept behind this book.

I believe wholeheartedly that there are moments, when playing in a band that is leading worship, that you break into another spiritual dimension and it can beat the feeling of any gig. Those moments are overwhelming and are hard to describe; in some cases, my body has gone numb and I've been holding back tears. It is an amazing experience that happens when you truly give yourself to what you are doing as a drummer.

WHO?

Do you play drums in your church or would you like to one day? Do you lead worship in your church and want to communicate, play, and worship better with your drummer?

Then this book was written specifically for you!

This book was designed for the individuals who are serving in their Churches by drumming in the worship teams! Young or old, professional or beginner, megachurch or small hall, contemporary worship or traditional hymns, in a team of drummers or the only one, a lifelong Christian or saved last week. This book is for you to put in your bag and use as a tool. It was specifically made to be an A5 size so that it can easily fit into a stick bag or backpack. The amount of information in this book should give you a helping hand in the majority of worship situations.

HOW?

The content of this book has been in the making for the past 12 years, that is a crucial piece of knowledge to hold onto. Like any craft, skill, or practice, it takes time and work to become proficient. So go easy on yourself! There is a lot of information on the following pages so you are not expected to memorise all of it after the first read. This book is specifically called a "Field Manual" because it is something that needs to be taken into the field with you! Keep this in your stick bag or backpack and refer to it if you need to.

As a drum teacher, I regularly try to move my students thinking away from "that was a mistake", and direct them to a mental attitude of "that was a learning moment". If something goes wrong during a service or rehearsal, that is when this book can help. Highlight what the problem was and find in these pages how to avoid it next time.

If you find yourself in a situation that is new and unknown territory, then open these pages and look for tips and advice. If your worship leader is asking for something different in your playing and you're not sure how or what to do, open these pages and find the practical information that can help. If your playing is solid but your spiritual walk is dry or worship is a struggle, then open these pages and find some testimony on worship struggles and processes.

THE AUTHOR

My name is AJ and I work as a professional musician and drum teacher. I spend the majority of my time gigging with a number of different bands and teaching for a variety of companies around Bristol. I am endorsed by Vic Firth Drumsticks as part of their Education Team and have an instructional drum book called *'The Drummer's Odyssey'* which received a 4/5 star review in Rhythm Magazine.

I am currently part of the worship team at Woodlands Church in Bristol and spend a lot of my time helping out other churches around the country at different events, conferences, and services. I owe a huge percentage of my musical education to the various churches I have played in over the last 12 years. Churches really are an amazing place for musicians to hone their skills and shape their musicianship.

Having played in the majority of church environments, I felt that the knowledge and experience I've acquired has not only helped my own playing but given me a passion to help other drummers who are serving the Churche. So whether it is denominational or non-denominational, your regular or an unfamiliar church, a congregation of 25 or 10,000, I am hoping this book can equip the Drummers to serve their churches in the best way they can.

If you have any questions or comments then please do not hesitate to get in touch! Please use my website for contact info and other general information about myself.

www.ajrousell.com

APPRECIATION

A big personal thank you to the following people who have helped out with this product in some way:

Esther Champion, Colse Leung, Mark Reid, Sol Hardy, Ian & Sarah Rousell, Mat Miles, Christian Cunningham, Joe Hardy, Tom Hayes, and Jay Cook. Also the many churches, musicians and worship leaders that I have come into contact with over the years. Every service has contributed in some way to this book.

All Graphics and Photography by Jo Rousell.

WELCOME TO "THE FIELD MANUAL FOR THE CHURCH DRUMMER"

*

"A FIELD MANUAL;
BECAUSE IT NEEDS TO BE TAKEN INTO THE FIELD"

"THIS INSTRUMENT THAT WE PLAY GOES BEYOND JUST HITTING SOMETHING WITH A STICK; IT IS A COMMUNICATION INSTRUMENT"

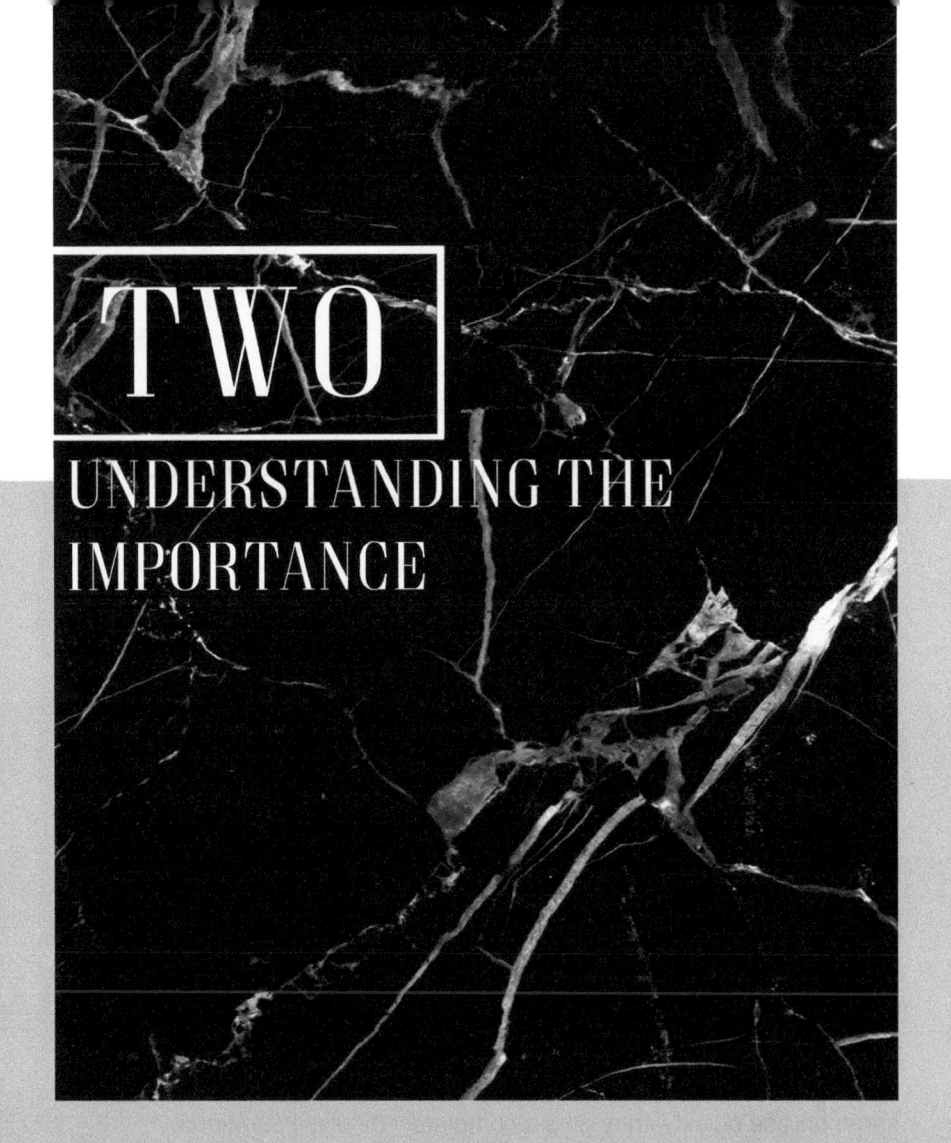

TWO
UNDERSTANDING THE IMPORTANCE

2
UNDERSTANDING THE IMPORTANCE
WORSHIPPING IS WHERE OUR WALK WITH GOD BEGINS, AND RHYTHM IS WHERE MUSIC BEGINS.

It could be argued (quite strongly) that everything musical essentially starts with rhythm. Rhythm is the basis of melody because for a note to have a start and an end point means that there is a rhythm involved. I have this beautiful mental picture of the first time that humankind picked up a stick and repeatedly hit it with another stick, and found amusement in it! Since then, rhythm has been used for a number of important, amusing, and fundamental things whilst becoming an integral component of our day to day lives.

Our basic communications and interactions are built around rhythm. If someone said a phrase slowly to you, and someone else said the exact same phrase quickly, they give a completely different emotional responses. "Can you come here?", can have very different connotations depending on the vocal rhythm used when speaking it. We have even developed a whole language built around rhythm; Morse Code was used throughout World War 2 to successfully communicate without the need for pitch or words.

When we look back through history, drums were one of the few instruments that were actually taken onto a battlefield because it evoked such an emotional impact, be it intimidation, motivation or inspiration.

This instrument that we play goes beyond just hitting something with a stick; it is a communication instrument that has been used for centuries to convey messages, emotional responses, and unifying actions. We can even go as far to say that at the very core of our being is an essential organ that pumps blood to the rest of our body using its own independent heartbeat. Even our physical bodies are reliant upon a rhythm to stay alive.

The concept that rhythm is so important for life and music is mirrored in the Churches relationship with worship. When they are combined, we have an unstoppable and spiritually powerful entity. Worship is something that is mentioned frequently throughout the Bible by Jesus, prophets, authors, and key figures. Worship is at the heart of our faith and is our outward expression of praise. I firmly believe that in everyone there is an inbuilt desire to worship, but sadly it can be misdirected and put onto other worldly things. "Let EVERYTHING that has breath praise the Lord", (Psalm 150:6) comes to mind when thinking about the important and integral nature of worship.

This book was written as a tool that is full of practical information for the Church drummers that are out there in various churches, which naturally means that a large percentage of these pages are filled with applicable and logistical advice. But all of that is irrelevant if the heart behind what we do as drummers doesn't line up with the spirit of worship. There is a passage in John that captures this perfectly; *"Yet a time is coming and has now come when the true worshippers will worship the Father in the Spirit and in truth, for they are the kind of worshippers the Father seeks. God is spirit, and his worshippers must worship in the Spirit and in truth.* (John 4:23-24).

This is WHY we do what we do as drummers! To anyone involved in worship there is a responsibility to remain humble while carrying a deep level of integrity. We have been put into a position of leading people to connect with their Father through musical worship, and that cannot be done if we give a half effort, or be done effectively without first understanding the importance of our role. So let's take a look:

WHERE WORSHIP AND DRUMS MEET

We use music in worship because music is such a powerful tool. It is no coincidence that there are countless songs surrounding love, heartbreak, anger, longing, and loss; simply because music can be one of the most effective mediums for expressing the emotions that are within us. It is why so many number one hits were by musicians writing songs for a lover; it is a direct expression of their love put into words and accompanied by melody.

When we look back at a number of historical shifts in culture and society, it is likely there was a band or artist also involved. Some iconic bands have been able to start a whole movement or revolution simply through the power of their message and the music they used to communicate it.

Therefore, it is no surprise that sung worship is one of the main avenues that we take to express our praise to God.

If we can see how important songs can be as a tool for worship and we have seen how important drums are to culture and music, then it is logical that the two work together. Once we really look into the impact that these two components can have, we can begin to view our time as a Church drummer in a very different way.

This instrument we play holds tremendous power, which therefore gives us great responsibility. *'A band is only as good as their drummer'* is a phrase that gets thrown around a lot, which can create two attitudes among drummers; 1) "Well I guess our band won't be very good if I'm all they have" or 2) "I now have a responsibility to be the best I can be! I have a reason to practice, I have a reason to serve, and I have a reason to pray for a blessing in this". There are many types of drummers spread among the churches ranging from professional drummers to hobby drummers.

Regardless of your skill level, your years/days of playing, the gear you have, or the amount of time you have spent practicing, we all fall into the same category when it comes to the Church. We ALL play an instrument that potentially carries monumental capability, and if we understand that and give it our best effort, our Churches will value what we are able to bring.

THE STARTING POINT

One of the things I love about being a drum teacher is that I am rarely surprised by how a student plays the instrument. Not regarding skill or technical ability, but by their mannerisms on the kit and how they subconsciously approach playing drums. This is because our drumming is always an outward expression of ourselves. It is rare to meet a drummer who has a bouncy, energetic, and hyperactive personality, whose drumming doesn't reflect that! Having spent countless hours watching videos of drummers online, it is so interesting to watch an interview with a drummer and then watch them play. Their playing always mirrors their personality. If their mannerisms are loud and excitable, or calm and docile, or quiet but confident, or even funny and cheeky, their drumming will always reflect those elements of their character.

This can even translate into our day to day emotional well- being. If you are enjoying a gig then you will play with more enjoyment, but if your mind is elsewhere then your drumming will be distant and disconnected. Having experienced countless gigs that have started with a received parking ticket, a confrontation from a rude punter, equipment that was unusable or just having a rubbish day overall, it is safe to say that it all genuinely affects your playing, and changes how you mentally approach the gig. (Although when standing in as the drummer for a metal band, that little bit of added aggression and angst came in useful…)

Taking this to another level, we need to be aware that spiritually this can also carry some weight. Some of my toughest Church services have been when I have been spiritually dry or running on empty. Losing sight of why we are there, taking for granted that we are leading people in worship, being self-indulgent, or not prioritising our spiritual walk are all backward steps that are so easy to fall into. Our drumming is a reflection of our inner self, so if we are not keeping our spiritual welfare healthy then our attitude and playing will subsequently suffer.

So where does this all begin? Like anything, it starts from the core. *"Do nothing out of selfish ambition or vain conceit. Rather, in humility value others above yourselves."* (Philippians 2:3) As drummers, our primary role is to serve and support our team of musicians and congregation, but we are also called to have a heart of worship in everything that we do.

Having spoken to many people with various professions, there are those who have an incredible attitude towards worshipping through everything they do. If they work on the tills at a supermarket, they believe that they should be the best they can be at that job, which in turn becomes part of their worship. This is what we will be looking into throughout the following chapters; how we can give our best to our Church as an act of personal worship so that we can be worship-filled, humble, and skilled drummers.

*

"I AM CONVINCED THAT SOMETHING IN THE ATMOSPHERE OF WORSHIP CAN DRAMATICALLY SHIFT WHEN THE MUSICIANS ARE GIVING THEIR BEST"

THREE

GIVING YOUR BEST

THE FIELD
MANUAL

3
GIVING YOUR BEST

"In the course of time Cain brought some of the fruits of the soil as an offering to the Lord. And Abel also brought an offering—fat portions from some of the firstborn of his flock. The Lord looked with favour on Abel and his offering, but on Cain and his offering he did not look with favour." (Genesis 4:3-5)

So you have found yourself in a position where you are playing drums at your Church. GREAT!

It's a genuine privilege to lead worship in any situation and that is something to never forget, regardless of how long you have been playing or how many services you have under your belt. This attitude should always be there and will be at the core of how we approach everything from here on out. The story of Cain and Abel is so important to revisit from time to time, especially for musicians. Cain brought his minimum requirement to the Lord, whilst Abel brought his absolute best! God looked on Abel's offering with favour whilst rejecting Cain's. God doesn't ask us to bring something that we are not able to give, but he does ask that we give him everything. He is worthy of the best of what we have regardless of its grandeur. It is an attitude of the heart rather than of physical contributions.

Coming from the previous chapter which was surrounding the spiritual aspects of why we do what we do as drummers, the following chapters focus on the practical and logistical elements. A Bible verse that I believe every member of a church music team should have engrained into their minds is Colossians 3:23 *"Whatever you do, work at it with all your heart, as working for the Lord, not for human masters"*. I have this verse engraved on a plaque, which is on one of my favourite Snare Drums because I feel it is so crucial to remember when serving in any capacity. 'Giving your best' is a way of honouring God and his Church, so when we serve by drumming, it is important to not give half an effort. When we find ourselves in a position of leading people in worship, this attitude HAS to be there. I'm convinced that something in the atmosphere of worship can dramatically shift when the musicians are giving their best musically, spiritually, and mentally! It can be truly special.

This chapter focusses on the HOW. How can we practically get the best out of our equipment, the best out of the pre-service process, the best sound from the kit, and give our best to our worship teams? All of these aspects are what happens behind the scenes and are all part of our personal worship as drummers.

GENERAL ETIQUETTE

Being a drummer that other musicians enjoy playing with, and want to play with again, can involve a lot more than just our drumming. There are so many contributing factors that dictate whether a drummer gets called back again, and a lot of these factors are demonstrated before they have even picked up their sticks! They are elements that surround character, respect, etiquette, and personalities. The definition of 'etiquette' is "the customary code of polite behaviour in society or among members of a particular profession or group". This goes beyond just having decent table manners, it is meant to make everyone feel comfortable and at ease.

This portion of the "Giving your best' chapter looks at ways of conducting ourselves as drummers so that we can honour and serve our Church and worship teams.

HAVE GREAT TIMING

Having good timing as drummers transcends so much further than whether we speed up when we play. It applies to our punctuality and reliability as musicians, which is no different to the 'not-church' music industry. There is a great quote that drummers have used when talking about auditions or general gigging; *"If you are early then you are on time, if you're on time then you're late, if you're late then don't bother"*. Now obviously, it's an extreme. If you happen to be running late, don't just go home! Otherwise it is guaranteed that your Church will never ever use you again. It is still a good attitude to hold in our minds.

I have seen more musicians not be called back simply because they are regularly late and unreliable; sadly, they were usually amazing players as well. Good punctuality is a way of honouring your music team, respecting the Church service you are playing in, and building a good reputation for yourself. It also results in so much more grace from your worship leader on the rare occasions you are late for reasons outside of your control. Even when you are in the building, having good punctuality involves being on stage at the right time! Nothing is more awkward or irritating than a band who are ready to play, but are waiting for one musician who is somewhere in the building but not on stage… Don't be that person!

KNOW THE SONGS

PUNCTUALITY is the priority before you get to the Church, PREPARATION is the equivalent once you are in the building.

Being prepared usually boils down to the songs and the equipment. Do you know the songs you were asked to know, and do you have the equipment that you knew you had to bring? When the worship leader asks who has listened to the new songs, your hand should shoot straight up in the air with confidence! We explored in the previous chapter how important the drums are within musical contexts, so knowing what you are playing is vital to giving your best to your church music team.

There is no doubt that life can be busy, so even if you aren't able to learn the drum parts note for note, you can still listen to the song to understand the feel and vibe. If the drummer understands the style of the song, then you immediately have a solid foundation for the rest of the band to build on. It can be so much harder to get a whole music team on the same page if the drummer doesn't know what is going on.

LISTEN WHEN OTHERS ARE TALKING

This point is so important for showing respect and consideration to the rest of your team. Listening to others isn't just about daydreaming when they are talking to you; it is also about being respectful when other musicians are talking to each other.

One of the most frustrating scenarios in a rehearsal room is when two musicians are trying to sort something out and a different musician is playing because they are not directly involved in their conversation. Having an awareness of ALL of the team and what they are doing is so important. Even if someone is not talking to you directly, you can still learn and hear information that can be important to your role. Be aware of everyone in the team!

We play an instrument that can become very loud very quickly, so be considerate of your band members who are trying to talk to each other. This naturally transcends to when people are trying to talk to you! Don't noodle (playing on the kit, but nothing in particular) when someone is asking you something, and allow people to finish their sentences before jumping in with an answer or reaction.

These basic social etiquettes can go so far when wanting to keep a friendly team atmosphere and be a drummer that other musicians enjoy playing with.

BE EASY TO COMMUNICATE WITH

DEFENSIVENESS; This is something that can be a very natural human reaction when given feedback. It can be so natural that we sometimes don't even know we are doing it. Becoming defensive when someone appears to be (or is blatantly) criticising our playing is so common, but also something to actively fight against. One of the main dividers within music teams can be the differing of opinions, usually birthing from one musician commenting on another musician's playing.

Try to remain detached from defensiveness as it can become really toxic to your well-being and the teams morale. As tricky as this can be, try and take negative feedback as 'non-personal' comments so that it doesn't affect your character or confidence. As a quick side note, use wisdom and subjectivity in this. If the feedback you're being given is obviously designed to belittle or diminish your confidence, then that's a whole different ballgame. As a general rule, being a drummer that is easy to communicate with and discuss ideas with can be what makes you a joy to work with.

Worship Leaders usually have an idea in their head of how they would like the music to sound, so if they are asking for something different from you then avoid a defensive attitude and adopt a serving mindset to give them your best.

LEARN HOW TO TALK TO OTHERS

To keep this point short and direct, there is one thing to avoid when communicating with your musicians: ACCUSATION. Always be thinking about HOW you are wording something when you are giving feedback to others. It's not uncommon for some musicians to be a tad sensitive or defensive, so the less 'accusation' in your feedback the better. The difference between "Why are you playing that section so fast?" compared to "Did you want to go faster in that bit or keep it the same speed?" are polar opposites, but get the same point across.

The first one pushes blame and fault, the second is communicational and is searching for a team solution. It is a simple piece of advice, but truly works wonders at keeping morale high and relationships intact. There can be a lot more psychology involved in your church worship team than what is apparent and obvious. It is so important to be discerning and wise in how we communicate with others.

GETTING THE BEST FROM YOUR EQUIPMENT

The gear that we WANT to use, the gear we LIKE to use, and the gear we HAVE to use are three very different things. A drummers' expectation of 'good gear' is usually at a heightened level due to the hours spent reading equipment reviews, watching incredible drummers using top of the range gear, and browsing drum shops for the latest releases. In reality, a large percentage of churches simply do not have a budget that allows them to grant their drummers their unlimited equipment specifications. If we were given our churches bank card and a large drum store, then spending a few thousand pounds on a dream set up would be incredibly easy for us. Sadly, this is merely a dream that will be very unlikely to happen.

So we have two choices as drummers who have a spirit of 'giving our best': We can either complain about how the equipment we have is not as good as it could or should be, or we can praise God that at least we have gear that we are free to use to the best we can. Obviously it is good to use wisdom in this; there is a difference between just being negative and expressing constructive criticism about a piece of equipment that is literally unusable… So if we are building a culture within the musicians of the Church that are 'giving their best', how can we do that regarding the drums and equipment we have available? If we play at a Church whose kit is just about usable, are we destined to spend every service grimacing while we play it?
NOPE, here are a few points that should help:

DECENT HEADS CAN MAKE CHEAP DRUMS SOUND GREAT

The drum kit is a fascinating instrument when you really get into the mechanics of how it works. One common misconception is that the actual shell of the drum is where ALL the sound and tone comes from. The shells are really important and the material used (Wood, Metal, Acrylic) contributes massively to the overall tone of the kit. It is incredible how a Snare Drum made from Maple Wood can sound so different to a shell made from Walnut Wood, especially when you play them side by side!

Yet one huge contributor to the overall sound of a kit that is easy to forget is the Drum Heads that we put on the drums. It is the equivalent of having a beautiful multi-thousand-pound guitar, but using spaghetti for strings and expecting it to sound good. The Drum Shell is the SOURCE, the Drum Head is the ACTIVATOR. A drum can only sound as good as the heads that are put on them. If your Church has a very mediocre drum kit, then invest in some seriously good drum heads to counteract it.

The market for Drum Heads can be a vast and overwhelming place to look into if you're not entirely sure what heads you need. To narrow this search down, there are basically two key elements to think about; whether the head is coated and the thickness of the head. Non-Coated Heads are completely clear, whereas Coated Heads have a textured finish on them. The coating is usually white, but some companies have released other colours. So the main difference is that Non-Coated Heads are transparent, Coated Heads are not. Clear Heads give the drum more attack and brightness, whereas Coated Heads are warmer and more rounded.

The thickness of Drum Heads usually comes in two forms; Single Ply or Double Ply. A 'Ply' is essentially a sheet of Mylar (plastic). If you put thinner Drum Heads on your kit then you will find a much brighter tone and a lot more sustain. Thicker Drum Heads are usually deeper with a lower tone, more punch, and more durability/longevity. Some heads also come with an extra ring installed so it adds some natural dampening to the head to cut out any unwanted over-ring.

So buying Drum Heads essentially comes down to knowing what combinations of these factors to go for. If you want your kit sounding bright and clear, then use some single ply Non-Coated Heads. If you want your kit to sound deep and warm, then use double ply Coated Heads. If you want your kit to sound huge with loads of attack, then use a double ply Non-Coated Heads. And so on and so on…

We live in a world nowadays with an almost unhelpful amount of selection, but this has also led to thousands of review videos online for Drum Heads. Pick the head you think will work and then search for reviews and demos to see whether it is the sound you are after. Enjoy the process, research reviews for heads and enjoy the process of taking a mediocre kit and making it sound exactly how you want it to!

MICROPHONES CAN ADD BODY

For small churches, there is no need to mic up every drum on the kit because the drummers' volume is usually the first thing to receive complaints. Cymbals are renowned for being able to really cut through a mix and be potentially difficult to control, so adding any overhead mics to this can just enhance the problem. Whereas, a Bass Drum emits a much lower frequency which will not be able to cut through the mix as much as the higher frequencies coming from cymbals. If you are playing in a small room, the only thing you really need to mic is the Bass Drum. It is amazing how much difference this can make!

The Bass and Snare Drum are the elements of a drum beat that keep the rest of the band together, so adding more 'depth' to your Bass Drum without boosting the other drums or cymbals can improve the overall sound instantly. If you have a hole in the front head of your Bass Drum, simply put the mic into the drum. The closer to the batter head you move the mic, the more attack and 'slap' you will get. A microphone in the middle of the drum, gently blended into the overall mix, can add that extra bit of body to the drum kit without having to spend hundreds of pounds on lots of different microphones.

EVERYTHING SOUNDS BOOMY & RINGY? DAMPENING CAN FIX EVERYTHING

This can be a common problem when playing a kit that is quite old and hasn't had the drum heads replaced in years. You hit a drum and the sustain lasts forever and really doesn't sound nice. Tuning can really help with this, but can be pointless when the heads are so old that all tone has long gone. To change all the heads on a kit can be expensive, so if this is an unavoidable problem, dampening is the next best step.

Dampening can come in many forms: Dampening Pads are little gel pads that stick to the drum head and kill off any 'over-ring' from the drums. The more dampening pads you put on a drum the more ring is removed. Duct Tape can also be used but is a nightmare to remove from the heads and also doesn't really allow the drum head to vibrate. This can ruin the sound entirely instead of just removing the unwanted overtones. Dampening Rings can be really effective though. These are clear plastic rings that you place on the drum to have a dampener that hugs the drum hoop, which deadens the sound and removes any unwanted tones.

Having a nice kit with decent heads that is well tuned is ALWAYS the first call to get a great drum sound. But as a last resort, when nothing else is working and the sound still isn't great, then dampen the heads. On the other hand, the Bass Drum can be really hard to control with no dampening at all. There are a number of famous drummers who don't dampen their Bass Drums at all and they sound great, but these drummers are amazing at tuning with a deep understanding of how a drum works.

As a general rule, a pillow inside the Bass Drum lowers the 'booming' tones and gives it more of a low end 'thump'. It will be easier to play, easier to mix and easier to control.

TUNING THE DRUM KIT

Just because a drum kit isn't considered a pitched instrument does not mean that it requires no tuning at all. When playing with multiple pitched instruments (piano, guitar, bass, oboe, banjo, harp, glockenspiel, kazoo etc…) being in tune is really important to ensure that all the notes that are being played are at the same tonal pitch to avoid any nasty clashes. As drummers, it is incredibly rare to tune our kits to the key of a specific song, as tuning a kit can take a while and it isn't practical to do it between every song. That does not mean that tuning our kits becomes irrelevant, it just means that how and why we tune a kit comes from a slightly different perspective.

It is rare (but not unheard of) to tune a drum kit to a specific pitch or key, but because the key of each song can vary multiple times throughout a worship set, it would be a waste of time. So, the number one aspect of tuning a kit is to get the sound that best fits your worship team and the church venue. The difference between a well-tuned kit and a un-tuned kit can be colossal, so in order to give our best to our church, it is wise to try and get the drum kit sounding the best we can.

Tuning a drum kit well is a real art, and some drum techs spend hours practicing it so that they can get the exact sound that they are looking for. It really is amazing to watch a true drum tuning guru at work making a kit sound phenomenal. However, not all of us have invested as much time into enhancing our tuning skills as we could have, so to narrow down the vast amount of tuning possibilities, here are just three primary drum sounds that are easily available:

1. SAME PITCH

The two main contributing factors to the note produced by a drum is the Batter Head (the one you hit with a drumstick) and the resonant head (the one under the drum). More specifically, it is the relationship between these two heads that heavily dictates the sound produced when you strike the drum. The first option for tuning a drum is to have both heads tuned to the same pitch, which will create a single note/tone when played that will have a lot of sustain.

2. PITCH BEND (DOWN)

This tuning method creates a different tone to the previous option and creates a sound where the drum 'dips' in pitch after striking it. To achieve this, the batter head needs to be tuned to a higher note than the resonant head.

The resonant head (bottom head) determines the pitch that the drum will finish on, whereas the batter head (top head) will determine the pitch that the drum starts on when struck. So tune the resonant head to the desired note, and then tune the batter head to the same note and then raise it a little more!

3. PITCH BEND (UP)

Exactly the same principle as the downward pitch bend, but this time you mirror the tuning of each head. For a pitch bend that sharpens, you will need to tune the batter head to a higher pitch than the resonant head. It makes a huge difference which pitch bend you choose, so have fun experimenting and seeing what works for you and what doesn't!

QUICK & EASY STEP-BY-STEP TUNING GUIDE

We quickly covered the three main options for how to tune a drum. The logical next step is to give an overview of how to actually make the drum do what you want. It can be dead simple when condensed into this short step-by-step guide:

1. Loosen all the lugs (screws)
2. Remove the Drum Hoop
3. Place a new Drum Head on the Shell (make sure the logo is at the top otherwise it will annoy you every time you look at it…)
4. Place the Drum Hoop back on top of the Drum Head and realign all the lugs
5. Using your fingers, tighten each lug until you cannot tighten any more. (This is what is referred to as being tuned 'Finger Tight'.)
6. Using a Drum Key, turn each lug a half rotation. Do not go around the drum in a clockwise direction! Turn one lug, then turn the lug opposite, then move to the next lug, then turn the one opposite, and so on. Not going round in a clockwise direction means that the Head will be being tightened evenly. The tighter the lugs, the tighter the head will be, but ensure they are all the same for a consitent tone.
7. HIT THE DRUM! If you like how it sounds then leave it where it is, but if you're not enjoying what you are hearing then start tweaking. Your ears are your number one tool when tuning, so keep tightening or loosening all the lugs until you are happy, and then stop!
8. If you are changing the heads on your Snare Drum, then a good rule of thumb is to tighten the bottom head as tight as you can! This means the snare wires have a tight surface to vibrate against, so you'll get lots of clarity from your ghost notes.

THE MOST EFFECTIVE ORDER TO TUNE THE LUGS:

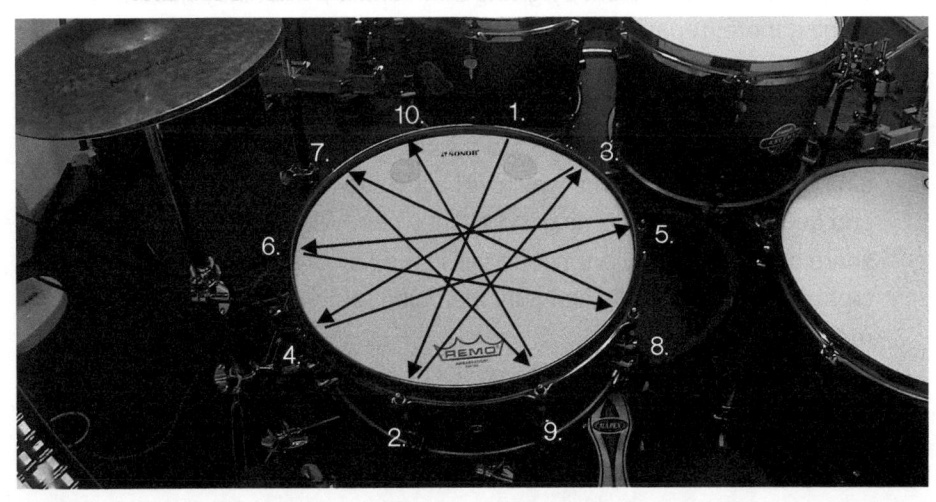

SOUNDCHECK ETIQUETTE

There is an art to sound checking well, and there is an element of 'etiquette' when doing so. 'Sound Check Etiquette' is there in order to make the sound engineers job as easy as possible, and to not irritate every other member of the band. To add a personal note to this point, I have to regularly remind myself of the following points, as they are so easy to slip away from.

So try hard to keep true to these tips and everyone's sound-check, including yours, will be so much smoother.

YOU ARE NOT BEING ASKED TO SHOW OFF YOUR CHOPS AND LICKS

So so so many drummers use the sound-check as a time to "rip it" on the kit. Demoing that new fill or mental groove that they have been working on, or even using it as a chance to solo and musically vomit over the kit (Be honest, we've all done it....). Now although this is fun, and appeals to our inner-drummer, it is a sound engineers worst nightmare.

Their job is to get the overall band sounding as good as they can, so the sound-check is the first step of that process. Make the sound-check as easy as you can for them by giving them exactly what they need and nothing more; repeated single strikes of a drum until they ask for something else.

By striking the drum once you are giving them a clear indication of the tone that the kit is making, which will allow them a chance to EQ it well and get the kit sounding as good as they can. When asked to "play the snare drum", so many drummers will immediately start drum rolls, flam taps, double stroke rolls and mini marching routines, which can all be really unhelpful.

The sound engineer doesn't need a wall of notes thrown at him to get a good sound out of the kit. Keep it dead simple and allow them to hear the tone of the drums clearly by playing one clear hit and then repeating.

IF YOU'RE NOT BEING ASKED TO SOUNDCHECK, THERE IS NO REASON TO PLAY

One thing to always remember for ANY musical setting that you find yourself in is that you are not the only person involved. If there is another musician on stage with you, then you both need to be considerate and be thinking of the others beside yourselves. One key way of demonstrating this attitude is by showing some courtesy while other musicians are sound checking.

A huge irritation for a sound engineer is when trying to check the levels and tone of one instrument, but not being able to hear them clearly because another instrument is 'noodling'. The term 'noodling' is basically musician lingo for that person who just sits with their instrument, constantly playing something, in their own little world, oblivious that something else might be happening. If you are not being asked to play, then don't. Give the other musicians space to sound-check and the whole process will run so much smoother and be over quicker.

This is a serious discipline though! As drummers it is natural to want to play our instrument, which is why noodling is such a common problem and argument-starter in rehearsals. So like breaking any habit, addiction or natural compulsion, the initial temptation needs to be removed. When you are not being asked to play, put your sticks down on your snare and take your feet off the pedals.

By distancing yourself slightly from the kit you will lessen the temptation to play it. It is a small point, but something that can dictate whether a sound engineer likes it when you're on the team or not...

BE CLEAR AND POLITE ABOUT WHAT YOU NEED

Getting the levels right in your monitor can be a tricky task anyway, but add poor communication as well, and you have an impossible situation. Being clear about what you are asking for is essential, and can come down to a few methods of communicating. If the room you are playing in is small enough to talk to the sound engineer, then being polite and respectful when asking for a level change is the way to go.

Never demand anything; having a respectful and polite nature can be the catayst for whether you put someone on edge or not. If you are in a room where talking to the sound engineer isn't practical, then hand signals are the next best thing, but it is essential that you are clear.

Simply pointing to the worship leader and then pointing to your monitor means jack all... Are you saying you want more or less of their voice? Or that you want more or less Guitar?? Or are you saying you can't hear anything at all??? Or are you saying the general volume is too loud??? Be clear about what you want!

So, time to imagine a realistic and believable scenario.
Let us picture that common development that we find ourselves in where the mix is great but we are struggling to hear the worship leader's vocals enough.

Here is a step by step guide to successfully giving a CLEAR non-verbal request to the sound engineer.

1. **WAVE** (You need to get their attention so they are looking at you)
2. **POINT TO THE WORSHIP LEADER** (Highlighting which instrument will need to change)
3. **POINT TO YOUR MOUTH** (Signalling that it is a vocal issue, not a guitar issue)
4. **POINT TO YOU MONITOR** (Signalling that the problem is with your personal mix)

5. **WITH THE OTHER HAND, POINT UPWARDS** (Signalling that the volume needs to increase)
6. **THUMBS UP WHEN YOU ARE HAPPY** (signalling that the level is now what you need)

This is a great example of using non-verbal communication to let a sound engineer know what you would like changing. Some of us are useless at lip-reading (I am literally useless at it), so if that is the case, use clear hand signals.

So the prep has been done, which leads nicely into the next chapter that talks about the 'Pre-Service' motions and experiences.

*

'...IT CAN BE SO EASY TO FORGET THAT MUSIC IS A REAL OUTWARD EXPRESSION OF OUR INNER SELVES.

FOUR

PRE SERVICE AND THE BAND

4
PRE-SERVICE & THE BAND

In order to give YOUR best, it can sometimes involve finding the best in OTHERS.

"For just as each of us has one body with many members, and these members do not all have the same function, so in Christ we, though many, form one body…" (Corinthians 12:12 NIV)

Musicians can be a fun bunch of people, but it can be so easy to forget that music is a real outward expression of our inner-selves. The reason this is important to remember is because a musician's character and personal mannerisms are usually always present within their playing. There are a lot of mental and psychological elements to being a musician, and as Christians playing in a worship team, this can sometimes be reflected in our spiritual-self. *'Getting the best out of a band'* sounds like a job for a worship leader or Musical Director, not the job for the drummer sat at the back of the stage.

I would respectfully disagree…

As musician's, it is all of our duty to play the best we can, and as Christians it is our calling to glorify Christ in everything we do. The two go hand in hand, which is why it is crucial not to become too 'self-involved' as a musician. It is your role as a drummer to hold the rest of the band together. Therefore, it can also become your role to sometimes adjust your playing in order to bring out the best in the other musicians. There are various ways of doing this, which will be covered in more detail later in a chapter titled "In the Field." For now, this chapter covers the practicalities of working within a church band before the service has begun. It also considers how to be a drummer that musicians like to work with, who gives their all in their drumming, and brings out the best in the band as a whole.

READING THE SOUNDCHECK & PRACTICE TIME

Soundchecks are primarily there to test stage volumes, monitor levels, check whether the band sound good together, and whether everything is comfortable. But the soundcheck can be more than that. This will be the first time that you make noise with these musicians, so use it as an opportunity to analyse who you are playing with, how everything clicks together, and how the worship leader does their thing.

TESTING OR NOODLING...

Noodling: *"to improvise or play casually on a musical instrument"*
Sounds quite nice when its worded like that doesn't it? Yet in reality, it is not... It is annoying and shows that you are either bored, showing off, or in a world of your own. There is a difference between noodling and testing the kit/checking the positioning of your instrument. The reason noodling is annoying is simply because we play a loud instrument. It is tough to noodle quietly on a drum kit, which can become irritating when other musicians are trying to discuss something, or the sound guy is trying to get levels for the other instruments.

Building a habit of being a 'non-noodler' can be invaluable and comes down to one simple action; as soon as you have established that the drum kit works and you can reach everything, put your sticks down. If your sticks are in your hand then you WILL play the instrument because it's fun and we love it! Take away temptation and show respect for the rest of the team.

YOUR LEVELS

How much control you have over your monitor mix is heavily subjective depending on the church you are playing in. Some churches have really upped their game and gone all out, ensuring their musicians have individual mixers to control what they can hear. Whereas, some churches have no such luxury so need to have a sound engineer at the desk taking requests from the band, as well as mixing the front of house sound.

If you have little control over your mix, then you need to accept from the word go that it isn't going to be perfect. Your mix is in the hands of someone who can't hear it in the same environment that you are hearing it, so trying to be too precise and constantly asking for minor alterations to get the perfect mix will take forever, most likely leading to frustration. It becomes about prioritising rather than personal preference.

Here are the priorities: Main Vocals, Acoustic Guitar, and Bass. These need to be the loudest in your mix if you do not have full control over the levels; everything else is a bonus. Most likely, the Keys and Electric Guitars are only essential in the intro to a song, so as long as you can hear their tempo you should be fine. If you have them all in your mix at full volume, it can start to sound muddy and packed, which can actually make it harder to hear any clarity.

If you have full control over your own mix, with any number of the apps and mixers available nowadays, then altering your monitor levels effectively can make the world of difference. The priority instruments are still the focus, but you can also have the other instruments lower in the mix so that you can pick them out when you need them. If you have the ability to pan certain channels (choose whether they come through your left headphone, right headphone or both), then I suggest mixing them so that it matches where the musicians are on stage.

If the bass player is on my left, I pan them into my left headphone, if the keys player is on my right, I pan them right, and if a singer is stood in front of me, I keep them centred. It's perfection, but is also rare, and isn't to be expected all the time.

A SHORT PENCIL IS BETTER THAN A LONG MEMORY

This is something my Granddad used to say all the time when he would talk about the various Brass Bands he played for. The more songs within a set, the less reliable our memories become. Whereas charts and notes are not affected by this! The more you notate, the less chance there is of forgetting something. There are certain things that are crucial to remember including whether you are counting the band in for a song, section changes, and the specific groove if it is key to the song.

Some churches that have a music team full of seasoned musicians can start to try new things and move away from the standard ways of playing well known tracks; it is at this point that memory can begin to be tested. Just write it all down, and have a quick glance as and when you need to. It is better to have some notes there and not use them, than realise your mind has gone blank and you have nothing written down.

Most of the time writing notes down actually ingrains the information into our memories more, but if you do forget, then having a little reminder is all that is needed. If the drummer knows what is happening, it is a lot easier for the rest of the band to jump on board and be carried. If the drummer keeps missing cues, sections, and general parts, it can be devastating.

There is no shame in using a chart, but if it is something you are trying to keep on the down low then just be subtle! Seeing a drummer looking down is not uncommon, and congregations do not need to know that there is a piece of paper on the floor telling you what to do.

HOW DOES THE WORSHIP LEADER COMMUNICATE?

Although there are general mannerisms and signals, you will notice slight variations as you play with more worship leaders. The main thing to watch is how they signal section/dynamic changes, and how much time they give you to make those changes. Some worship leaders signal half a beat before they want to make a change, whilst others seem to give a full 16 bars! Some worship leaders are fairly predictable, whist others have a certain "curveball" nature about them.

All these extremes can be tricky, so it is good to understand what is going to be expected. Figure out early on whether they let you know what is happening with hands signals, or with foot actions, or with the positioning of their instrument, or whether they even communicate at all!

There is no shame in asking what certain signals mean to double check that you understand how that specific worship leader communicates. There are few things more awkward than when a leader has signalled for the drums to stop by stamping their foot, but in your past experiences, a stamping foot means "give it some beef!". The results can be interesting to say the least…

USE THE FIRST FEW SONGS TO BUILD TRUST

When drumming in a worship band, all anyone wants is a dependable, consistent rock to use as a strong foundation (cheeky parable reference). Your tempo needs to be solid, your groove needs to be confident, and your feel needs to be appropriate. The first full run through of a song is your chance to build this trust with your fellow musicians; so, no flashy fills and no super-techy grooves.

Keep it simple and solid, so that the band instantly relax and know that they can rely on you to keep everything together. No one cares how fast we've managed to get our right foot or how our new modulating paradiddle groove gives an implied polyrhythmic pattern that goes over

the bar line. Play as if there isn't a single drummer in the room that you need to impress, and all the other musicians will like you more.
Simple as.

FIGURING OUT THE TEMPO IS ALWAYS INTERESTING…

Every musician has a slightly different 'inner-metronome'. It is very rare that anyone naturally has a phenomenal "to-the-click" perfect timing. The majority of us will either naturally speed up or slow down when we play. This can be even more apparent in Worship Leaders and the tempos that they like songs being played at. Every Worship Leader has a slightly different "inner-pulse", and it isn't uncommon to play the same song at slightly different speeds depending on who you are playing with. Know the tempo of the song, but be prepared for a worship leader to ask for it to be slightly slower or faster.

If you are playing in a church with multiple worship leaders, it is a good idea to try and remember who likes the songs slightly faster or slower. Some worship leaders openly acknowledge and admit that they like playing the songs at a slightly different tempo. However, some aren't aware they are doing it. Be flexible and responsive to what they are asking. This is a real opportunity to develop a pride-less attitude as a drummer, which is demonstrated in the way that we work with the rest of the team.

It can be a really tough situation when you know the tempo is right, but you are being asked to play it differently.

CARS HAVE INDICATORS, BANDS HAVE DRUMMERS

Subtle things that drummers do can give other musicians reassurance that what they think is about to happen, is actually going to happen. The more relaxed a musician feels when they play with you, results in a more comfortable and trusting atmosphere towards the music as a whole. Watching a band full of musicians that are on edge and stressed is a really ugly environment to be in.

As the drummer, one of your most important roles regarding musical delegation is to relax the rest of the band, and allow them all to rest on your timing and groove. Reassuring the rest of the band that you are aware and involved in what is coming next in the song is a great way of creating a comfortable and 'surprise-free' environment.

Small dynamic changes to your playing, such as loosening the Hi-Hats a few bars before the chorus, gives a sense of comfort among the other musicians that you are all on the same path. Even eye contact is such a simple tool, but so effective for giving the band a mental 'thumbs up' for whether you are all at the same place in a song. Playing small fills, using Crash Cymbals to signal a new section, lowering your whole kit volume in a verse, moving to the Ride Cymbal when you enter the chorus, and building on the Toms to hit a loud section, are all super effective at giving other musicians warning for what is coming, or reaffirming where you all are in the song.

THE FOUR BASS PLAYERS

From day one of playing with other musicians in any environment or musical setting, drummers have had the same message drilled into their minds; the Drummer and Bass player need to be tight. This is also the only partnership within a band that is given its own name; The Rhythm Section. It is where the groove, power, feel and tempo of a performance comes from. It could even be argued that this collaboration of rhythmic musicians could also make or break the sound of a band.

Because of this, a band can only sound as tight as their rhythm section.

Understanding the importance of gelling with your bass player is all well and good; but what do we do as drummers when we work with a number of different bass players? Many of which we may not play with regularly? How do we ensure we are getting the best from each other and providing the best for the other musicians involved? What mindset should we have when playing with a new bass player?

From personal experience, there are primarily four types of bass players, and knowing how to adjust your drumming in order to play effectively with each one will ensure the overall sound of your band is still great.

1. The FOLLOWER
"a person who admires and supports a particular person or set of ideas"
These bass players listen to what you are playing and immediately get on board, syncing their playing to your kick drum almost too much. Be aware that what you now play will affect what they play, therefore affecting the overall sound.

So, you need to be thinking about how your drum part is going to affect their bass line and rhythm.

2. The INDEPENDENT
"Free from outside control; not subject to another's authority"
A bassist who is in their own zone, playing their own thing, but at least is solid and readable. There is a clear pattern and rhythm in their playing that is easy to hear. It is now your job to follow what they are playing and choose which of their notes to emphasise.

You need to sync your playing to what they are doing so that the overall sound is tight and together.

3. The ENGIMA

"a person or thing that is mysterious or difficult to understand"
Unpredictable, no repeating rhythm, long bass fills in random places, overplaying the simplest songs, no awareness of the other musicians. These bass players can be interesting to play with… What do we do when there is no predictability anymore?

Your job is to play the absolute bare minimum in your grooves. It becomes about just giving them as much space as you can to do whatever they seem to feel is 'appropriate'. It is annoying, but the overall sound of the band will be better(ish) if you step back and stay out of their way. If you try and match their intensity or align your playing with their lack of consistency, then the overall sound will be messy and anxious.

4. THE COMPANION

"a person with whom one spends a lot of time with or travels with"
If any bass players happen to be reading this chapter, then THIS is now your goal as a musician. This is hands down our favourite kind of bass player, and they are a dream to perform with!

In order for an individual to be considered a 'companion', there needs to be communication, trust, and respect, and this is exactly what is found in this style of bass player. You will find they listen to you, engage with what you are playing, and are easy to sync up with because they are clear and consistent in their bass lines.

If you can develop this style of relationship with your bass player, then the worship team you are in will be eternally grateful to you both.

TEMPERAMENTAL TEMPO

The hills are alive… with the sound of a solid, consistent, and metrically accurate pulse.

The big topic: TEMPO. It's interesting when looking at the definition; *"The speed at which a passage of music is or **should** be played at"*. 'Should' is the word that causes drummers, bassists, worship leaders and all musicians to laugh slightly. Usually because it brings immediate flashbacks of when the tempo definitely was not what it should have been during a song. The speed a song is meant to be played at, and the speed that it actually gets played at, can sometimes become two different worlds! Hilariously frustrating…

To put it plainly, when we really boil down what is actually important about our overall drumming, it is our tempo. Everything that we play as drummers is all based around the concept of speed, time, and pulse. We can spend years learning amazing drum grooves, staggering fills and complex patterns, but if we can't play any of it in time then it is all worthless. In the same fashion, if we memorise a songs drum parts perfectly but count the song off (the big clicks we do at the start of a song) at the wrong speed then it is a massive waste. Some of the busiest session drummers in the world are hired because of their phenomenal timekeeping and control of tempo, so it is crucial to prioritise the accuracy and precision of our timing.

If any of us have seen the film '*Whiplash*' and experienced that very real and tangible tension during the 'not quite my tempo' scene, it can very quickly bring back that emotion of confusing frustration that we can all relate to. Although it's rare that a worship leader will launch a chair at their drummer (but never say never…) it can still be a tense and uncomfortable feeling when we just can't get the speed of a song right. But it is so so so common!

Some of the biggest problems I hear from both drummers and worship leaders consist of counting songs off, speeding up or slowing down during the song, and changing the tempo accurately between songs. As a collective of drummers we are definitely not alone in this. This is exactly why this section was put into the book; in the hope to shed some light and share some tips that can make your life as 'the band's timekeeper' easier.

Here are some ideas;

YOUR 'INNER-CLOCK'

So the phrase "inner-clock" sounds a bit daft… Admitted. But it is a great way of thinking about our timing as drummers, and more specifically how to adjust our playing to get the speed of a song right. Everyone has an 'inner-clock', or to put it more specifically, an inbuilt awareness of tempo. But this is the interesting bit, everyone's inner-clock is slightly different. This makes perfect sense when considering why some drummers seem to push faster when they play, while others seem to always drag the tempo back.

We all naturally have a different concept of time and tempo, and learning which tendency you gravitate towards is a great revelation and is nothing to be ashamed of. Are you a 'Dragger' or a 'Pusher'? Do you naturally speed up when playing to a click, or do you naturally slow down? Which one do you get asked by your worship leader the most often; "can we slow the tempo down a bit?" or "can we drive this song a bit quicker?".

Knowing which one you generally swing towards isn't something to be ashamed of. I can honestly say that I seem to have a tendency to drag the tempo back. Realising that led to an awareness that I usually need to count songs off slightly faster than I think it should be and deliberately push my tempo forward when I play.

Drummers who seem to have phenomenally perfect timing just have an intensified awareness of when they speed up or slow down, so having "great time" is definitely achievable. It is just about improving the quickness in which you notice your speed is changing. And as with all of our drumming issues, we gain this heightened awareness by practicing.

Practicing with a Click/Metronome is great for realising where your natural inner-clock sits when accompanying a solid pulse, and this can be the difference between accurately perfect tempo or inconsistently mediocre tempo. Check out Chapter 8 "*The Hybrid Drummer*" for some useful exercises for practicing with a Click.

WORSHIP LEADERS ARE NOT MADE IN FACTORIES

Now granted, worship leaders usually seem to dress the same, act very similar and like the same sort of songs, but interestingly they all have a different inner-clock just like us drummers. So sometimes it is possible that they will prefer songs being done at slightly different tempos. This can be tricky though for drummers who play with multiple worship leaders. Picture this example; you play 'Lion and the Lamb' in one service and nail the tempo, but then in the next service a different worship leader says it's far too slow… This happens quite frequently.

In all honesty, it can be frustrating and confusing but it is not uncommon. Everyone feels tempo slightly differently, and worship leaders are included in this.

So how do we fix this? The answer is simple; WE CAN'T.

It is about accepting that every worship leader will have a different concept of time/pulse and noting which worship leader likes certain tempos. It comes down to the different inner-clocks that we all have, and the artistic preference from a worship leader. In the past I've worked with some worship leaders who feel that the recorded versions of worship songs actually sound better live when the tempo is slightly different. So sometimes it's not even a reflection on you or your timing, but of personal artistic preference.

If you play in a church with multiple worship leaders, it can be a good habit to try and remember which leaders like the songs slightly faster, which ones like them slightly slower, and which ones like them exactly at track speed. If you can log this in your memory then there will be less tension when it comes to practicing with the band because you are already prepared that they will like their song speeds a certain way.

Although, this is not an excuse to avoid practicing your time keeping or tempo consistency! Your awareness and proficiency of tempo is there to aid your worship leaders, which can become tested when a request for a different tempo comes your way.

IF YOU CAN'T SING IT, THEN YOUR WORSHIP LEADER DEFINITELY CAN'T

It is not uncommon for drummers to avoid singing. We play an instrument that requires very little pitched melody, we are sat at the back of the stage, and sometimes we have enough to think about with our co-ordination without adding our voice into the mix. Having said all of that, if you are a drummer that can also sing, the demand for your services shoots up! Once I decided to start offering extra backing vocals at gigs, the phone definitely started ringing more. But if you are not a singer and don't really want to be then that's fine, but it is amazing how helpful the physical action can still be. The only difference will be whether you have a microphone to sing into or not.

The idea behind it is this; if you can't fit the lyrics in with the speed of the song, then your worship leader definitely won't be able to.

It can be such a helpful tool to put yourself into your worship leader's shoes and see whether you would be happy with the tempo or not. The best moment to use this technique is before the count-in and during the intro of a song. Usually the chords used in an intro are the same as another section of the song, so put yourself in the singers position and sing along during the intro to see whether it feels comfortable for you. If it doesn't then something needs to be adjusted.

To ensure an excellent tempo right from the start, sing a line or two quietly to yourself before you start counting in the rest of the band. This will really ensure that you have the tempo spot on right from the beginning.

AIR DRUMMING IS ACTUALLY HELPFUL!

A really common phrase that is heard a lot when talking about drummers and their speed is to "feel the tempo", and this point is a follow up to that. How do we "feel a tempo"? The first thing everyone needs to admit is that we all Air-Drum from time to time. Whether it is to our favourite song, because of the drum ideas in our head, or just because we are simply bored. Pretending we are playing an imaginary drum kit isn't just subjective to actual drummers or musicians, everyone does it!

This is usually because it can be quite fun, but it can actually be really useful. Air-drumming is still the physical movement of what you do when you are on a drum kit. So air-drumming the groove just before you count a song off actually gives your body one or two bars to really FEEL how a tempo will effect your limbs when you start playing. It helps your body to settle into a tempo, before you include any of the other musicians or make any noise. It sets you up better than just jumping straight in and hoping for the best.

It's like doing a warm up before you start a long distance run. It gives your limbs are chance to feel how an activity will affect your body before

53

you actually start doing it, and in this case it is feeling the pulse of a song before counting the rest of the band in. Even better is to combine this with the idea in the previous point about singing a line or two before the count-off. Air-drumming the groove while singing the first line of the song will drastically lessen the chances of getting the tempo wrong! Don't take forever though, I literally mean only a bar or two. And please be subtle; no stadium style, stick twirling, epically distracting air-drumming.

WATCH OUT FOR CLUES

In the same way that a security guard is constantly observing their venue surroundings to ensure that no accidents or incidents are brewing, we need to be watching for clues after we have counted a song off. Musicians are pretty good at showing in their facial expressions and body language whether the speed of a song is what they want. So if the tempo isn't right, you should be able to tell within the first few seconds of a song.

Watch the body language of the other musicians. Look out for stamping feet, which seems to usually mean speed up. Watch for the worship leader leaning back slightly, as this usually shows they want it all to slow down a bit. Even someone grimacing can give a good indication that the song has been started too fast or too slow. The sooner you can clock something like this, the sooner you can rectify the problem. The result is being able to solve the tempo issue before the song gets too far along.

It is all about keeping your head up and observing the reactions on stage. When a worship leader is bobbing along and smiling, it is a great feeling knowing you have got the speed spot on. A great little trick is to look at the Worship Leader's foot! So many musicians subconsciously tap their foot while they are playing and this can give a great indicator to whether your tempo is roughly in the right area.

USE A HELPING HAND... OR A METRONOME

Metronomes are great... but you sometimes have to learn to love them. They are the immovable timekeeper that constantly reminds us just how bad our timing can actually be. But they can also be that little helper that aids us in getting an intro spot on. If your church band play along with a click for the entirety of a song, then great stuff! The tempo will be perfect for the whole track because the whole band has a present reference. But if you don't use them for the whole song, you can still use one just to get the speed right before you count-in the first song.

When you get up on stage, just get a click next to you (get one that flashes if your church room isn't that big) and just watch it for a bar or two to get the right tempo in your head before you count the rest of the band in. Sometimes all you need is that little reminder to get the first song the perfect speed, which can then set the trajectory for the rest of the service. Nerves, adrenaline, uncertainty, tiredness, emotions, and coffee can all effect our timing, so there is no shame in having a quick glance at a click to ensure the tempo for the first count-off is on point.

YOU ONLY GET ONE SHOT AT A GOOD INTRO

I see this happen in a lot in churches and at gigs; drummers starting the count-off before they have the tempo set in their minds. The reason for this is the idea that we have to start the song as soon as we can to avoid any silence. So the tendency is that as soon as the host, pastor or worship leader has finished talking, we immediately start counting in. This is a natural reaction, but can cause problems...

The important thing to remember is that when there is silence on stage, and you are the reason for that silence, it can feel like a lifetime. But in reality it isn't as long as it feels, and the silence isn't as awkward as it may appear. Realistically, if you take an extra few seconds before starting the count-off, it doesn't actually sound as bad as we think it does. The issue when starting the count-off without fully knowing and feeling the tempo is the increased chance of the song starting too fast or too slow, which will then need to be fixed while everyone is playing. This can become even more evident when changing between songs. Counting off a song, playing it, finishing it, then needing to count off a new song can be a really tricky task. This is because we have to judge the speed of a new tempo in relation to the tempo we have just finished playing at…

The concept for this section is this; It is always better to take an extra second but get the tempo spot on, than to rush the count-off and have to try and rectify a whole band that are now playing too fast or slow. Take a deep breath, hear/sing the song your head, feel the tempo and then bring in the rest of the band. That extra second can be gold!

EVEN IF IT'S WRONG, AT LEAST SOUND CONFIDENT

This point is really important as it can really affect the feel of your playing, the overall sound of a band, and the level of stress your worship leader experiences when you are playing. This is an attitude rather than an exercise and it comes down to one crucial concept; CONFIDENCE.

Confidence: *"the feeling or belief that one can have faith in or rely on someone or something."* As drummers, this is very much a key component to our role in a band. It has been said already in this book about the importance of being that solid foundation that the rest of the band can build on, and yet so often our playing doesn't reflect that. It can become timid and shy when we are unsure about a tempo.

One of my good friends, Christian Cunningham, highlighted a great point while we were talking about starting the worship time in a church service. His insight was that *"…hesitancy or shyness can be a killer. Since we usually start with the bigger sounding songs, the drummer needs to commit to it right from the beginning otherwise that sense of "uncertainty" can spread across the band pretty quick."*

We play an instrument that rarely goes unnoticed, and yet we can sometimes play as if we don't actually want to be heard. This makes absolutely no sense when we look at the nature of a drum kit. We are going to be heard when we play, so we may as well play with confidence and conviction.

This can have an incredible reaction when something goes wrong during a set. The best way to approach that situation is this; It is easier to adjust the tempo of a song if you have got the whole band on your side. When something isn't quite right, people gravitate towards the individual that radiates confidence and a certain 'leadership' quality. When it comes to tempo and pulse, that is our job as the drummer. Confidence does not mean cockiness or arrogance, it is about committing to the Intro of a song and playing it like we mean it. If the tempo isn't right then you can begin adjusting and bringing the band with you.

If you creep into a song with timidness, uncertainty, and hesitancy then the rest of the band just won't feel confident in looking to you for a solution. This doesn't come down to volume or aggressiveness when you play, but it is about sounding confident when you play even if you are not. Only then can you take the reins and fix any tempo problems. Most worship leaders will hate me for saying this, but it can completely change our attitude for when we play live. Once a mistake has been made there is actually nothing you can to UNDO it. All you can do is adjust your playing after that moment has passed in order to CORRECT the mistake.

So if you are counting in a big intro, starting the song with a big drum groove, or end up getting something wrong, then at least commit to your playing and remain confident and aware throughout it. You can fix any problem after it has happened.

General rule; If you're going to play, then play!

*

"WE GO TO A GIG TO BE **ENTERTAINED** BY THE MUSICIANS PLAYING, WE COME TO WORSHIP TO **JOIN** WITH THE MUSICIANS **PLAYING** ..."

FIVE
IN THE FIELD

THE FIELD
MANUAL

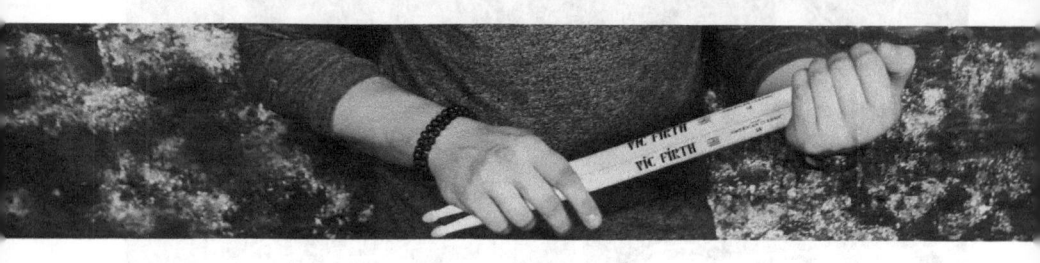

5
IN THE FIELD
THE LARGEST CHAPTER BY FAR; ESSENTIALLY ONE GIANT DRUM LESSON FOR THE CHURCH DRUMMER

For many reasons, leading worship is a really special and unique musical situation to be involved in. One key example of that uniqueness is that you are having to lead a room of people into a worshipful place, where they can meet with their Maker. Very few musical situations require giving the 'non-band-individuals' so much care, attention, and engagement. This goes beyond crowd interaction; here we have a responsibility to try take our congregations on a journey to worshipping God, which requires a large amount of forward thinking, observation, and openness to the spirit. The 'responsibility' is to take what we are doing seriously and give it our best. God is in the room from the begining and doesn't just show up if he approves of the songs we are singing. We don't have to use worship to earn his attention, but it is our role to try and create an atmopshere that helps our congragations meet with God.

This (in my humble opinion) is the key difference between worship and a gig. The reason I say 'key difference' is because there are actually a lot of unavoidable similarities between these two musical situations. If you look at a picture of both a Mega Church and gig at Wembley Stadium, or even a small intimate church and a small acoustic show, there are a lot of similarities. It can sometimes be impossible to even tell the difference between each picture unless being told which one is a gig and which one is a church. In both pictures you would see a band on stage with a crowd in front of them, usually with their hands up in the air.

The number one thing to keep at the front of our minds when we play is 'Why are we here?'. We go to a gig to be **entertained** by the musicians playing, we come to worship to **join** with the musicians playing so that we can all **communally** engae. Because of the existing similarities, it would be naive to think that the standard of musicianship plays absolutely no role in the possibilities available when a team lead worship. Giving our all in the situations we find ourselves in is a common preach for living a praise-filled lifestyle, which practically applies to worship.

Being the best you can by bettering yourself spiritually AND musically is so important in order to give more when you are 'in the field'. *Sing to Him a new song; Play skilfully with a shout of joy* (Psalm 33:3). Heart with no skill to support it has the potential to create an atmosphere that is hard or even impossible for the congregation to get involved with. Musical skill without a worshipful heart creates a self-indulgent concert. The importantance of our role as drummers has already been stressed a lot in the previous chapters. When the song starts and the hands start going up, we are all together and have one intention and purpose. The following points are all important in order to keep the musicians on the same page and to keep the worship from becoming a musical distraction for the congregation.

PLAYING IN CHURCH 101

So here it is, the largest chapter in the book and one giant drum lesson. Playing in Church is an ever-evolving state of worshipping our God whilst learning more about our instrument. Although this book will never match the personal touch of having private lessons with a drum teacher, there are some general tips, advice, and lessons that can be written down and applied to your drumming. Having lessons is always advised as it is so valuable to have your playing analysed and developed by someone who is in the same room as you. But this book was still designed as an effective tool to be used when needed.

Playing in Church 101; let's begin:

IF YOU DON'T WATCH AND LISTEN, THE BAND WILL STRUGGLE TO MOVE

Listening and watching for what could potentially happen on stage is an absolute must. Not doing this inevitably results in missing signals, misjudging a dynamic change or causing confusion on stage. Phenomenal musicians always give the same advice; communication when playing is everything. In order to communicate, you need to be aware of what is happening. In order to be aware, you need to be observant.

Listen to what the rest of the band are doing and how they are playing so that you don't miss anything! If the rest of the band have stopped playing and you're still ploughing away unaware, well that's just awkward for everyone. If you want the music to be dynamically interesting, tight and together, flexible to changes and responsive to decisions, then you need to always be listening and watching the team you are working with. Applying this mental state to any playing situation is so valuable when wanting to become a desirable/regualry called upon musician.

EVERY SERVICE CAN ESSENTIALLY BE A 'BOOT CAMP' FOR SESSION MUSICIANS

Every Worship Leader has a different 'vibe'. They can sometimes expect different things from the musicians they are working with and can all have a unique sound they are trying to capture. This can be the perfect training ground to prepare for the day you ever work with a Producer or Musical Director, and vice versa. The years spent playing in churches can prepare a drummer better than anything else for that first studio session. This is because of the countless Sunday mornings that consisted of giving a Worship Leader something unique. Being able to play a multitude of styles and genres is a great tool for playing in a band with creative leadership. Latin, Blues, Jazz, Pop, Dance, Hard Rock are all genres I have needed to be able to play at least once in a church. We hear the same songs a lot, so it is not uncommon for a Worship Leader to ask to rework a song slightly to give it some freshness.

UNDERSTAND THAT A SONG IS BIGGER THAN YOUR PART

Dynamics! Very few places educate you better on the effectiveness of dynamic playing than the music found in a church setlist. If you want to improve your ability to take a basic drum part and make it dynamically musical, then I'm sure you can guess by now where a good place to practice this is… Worship Leaders rarely ask for chops or overly flamboyant playing (sometimes they do in which case that's your green light to let rip), but more often than not they want the drums to be a foundation for the whole band.

Different songs call for different dynamics; energetic or reflective, quiet and loud sections, build-ups and accented phrases, etc. All of these will need to be drawn out using the varying dynamic range of our instrument. Think about the intensity of your playing and whether it fits the section that you are in. If you play at maximum volume and tone in the verse then you have nowhere to go for the chorus! Reflecting on my own playing when I was younger, I would regularly 'Max Out' dynamically in the chorus which would then give me nowhere to go in the Bridge. Usually, I would just beat the life out of the kit which just irritated the sound guy and congregation.

Picture having a half-full glass of water, and the fullness of that glass represents the 'dynamic state' of the song you are playing. If you start the song with half a glass full then you have the option to either add more water or take water out as the song progresses. If you start with a full glass then the only option for the entire song is to keep taking water out…

The folllwing section goes even further down the dynamic rabbit hole:

THE ART OF DYNAMIC PLAYING

Playing with dynamics can be one of the main contributors to whether or not your drumming is musical. When listening to any song, it is so rare to hear no dynamic changes at all. This is because it will create music that is boring, two dimensional, and lacks any interest or captivating qualities. Yet as drummers, it can be so easy to forget that dynamics within our playing are equally as important for bringing a song to life. This can go beyond just how loud or quiet we play; it can become a never-ending process that takes our thoughts to 'how' we play the drums, which part of the stick we use, which cymbal we use and what subdivision we're playing in.

When we play, it can be so easy and common for our focus to be on what would impress the other drummers in the room (we have all been guilty of this). It is completely the wrong attitude and can sometimes take years to learn that you are not playing in a band with other drummers, so the focus is all wrong. It is a sad day when we realise that no one else cares about our sick 32nd note linear fill we have been practicing for hours. Can you play musically, dynamically, and effectively? If not then you have just been given your new practice priority.

There is a really effective way of tuning our brains to think dynamically, that can even be practiced during a service or rehearsal. It is a simple yet great exercise; your task is to play a track and make the decision to only play groove or time. Everything has to be groove based, so no drum fills! The ONLY fill-like thing you are allowed to use is a simple build up, and that is only to be used occasionally! By making this decision, you are immediately forced to think about how your groove can lift and lower the dynamic range of each section of a song.

As drummers we naturally use fills to signal a section change and to show we are moving into a new part of the song. So how do we achieve the same result when we remove drum fills from our playing?? By making our overall drumming more dynamic! We will touch back on this later, but first let's look at ways of making our groove speak more musically. Here are some things to bear in mind:

WHICH PART OF THE STICK ARE WE USING?

If you use the Tip of the drumstick on top of a cymbal, it gives a completely different sound to if you use the shoulder of the stick on the side of a cymbal. Use the latter when you want to build excitement, tension, or to signal that a section change is coming.

Same goes for the drums! If you use the tip of the stick in the middle of the head, or use the body of the stick and hit the rim as well then you get two very different tones. This is the start of understanding the variety of tones and sounds that our instrument can produce. Sometimes it's not about adding more drums or cymbals, it is more about exploring the variety of sounds available with our minimal drum kits.

RIMSHOT OR NO-RIMSHOT?

A rim-shot is a way of playing your snare drum, which involves striking the drum head and the rim at the same time. This is a great tool for adding dynamics to your backbeat. Playing in the centre of the head will usually sound quite warm and blend into a mix better than a rim-shot, which is loud and has a lot more attack. It is possible and useful to mix them up though! If you use only one through a song you limit the amount of room you have to musically expand the various parts and sections.

Choose which sections to use rim-shots and you will see a noticeable difference in the dynamic range of your playing. A general good rule is in the sections that need to be strong and powerful (usually intro's, choruses, bridges or outro's) use a rim-shot on your backbeat; the quiet sections that still require a groove (verses, quiet bridges) use the tip of your stick in the centre of the head.

WHICH CYMBAL?

As drummers, we have the joy of being able to constantly add instruments to our kit! This can sometimes make a drum kit very 'cymbal heavy', so for this point we will narrow it down to just three; Hi-hat, Ride, and Crash. Choosing which cymbal to use can drastically change the sound or tone of a section. When a Hi-hat is closed it has a short and tight sound, whereas when it is open it has a lot more presence and power. When playing the Ride cymbal, think about where you are hitting it and with which part of your drumstick.

Using the tip anywhere on the Ride will sound thinner and more subtle than if you use the shoulder of the drumstick. The bow of the Ride cymbal produces long notes that ring out and add more 'body' when compared to a closed Hi-hat. However, the bell of the Ride cymbal still sounds full but decays quicker and has a harsher tone that cuts through a mix more. Crash cymbals are great but can also be the monster of the drum kit.

Being aware of the velocity that you hit these cymbals can completely change your overall kit sound. If you crash onto them they will cut through; how hard you hit depends how deafening they can be. You can also play a Crash on top with the tip of the stick like Ride cymbals which will give you a lighter tone than the Ride would give you.

HOW OFTEN ARE WE CRASHING?

Here is a really effective attitude to bear in mind whenever we are playing; The more frequently you use a Crash cymbal, the less impact it has. Crash cymbals (when used well) have so much impact and power. They work brilliantly for marking the start of a new section, accenting phrases, showing where the '1' is in a bar, and for finishing epic drum fills. All of those scenarios for a Crash cymbal to be used a valid, but it can become so easy to develop a default habit of using them too frequently.

A metaphor for emphasising this point is this; We all know those people in our lives who have a hideous temper and are quick to fly off the handle. The frequency of them losing their temper is predictable and something that we can become accustomed to. Whereas, we may also know people who rarely lose their temper and the majority of the time are placid and calm. When looking at these two types of characters, although it's never pleasant when someone loses their temper, how much more of a dramatic impact does it have when someone you never see angry suddenly erupts? It has more impact because it is rare, infrequent, and unexpected.

The same goes for Crash cymbals! If we use them every 4 bars, after every fill, at the start of every section and to signal the start of every groove, then we drastically minimise the potential impact that the cymbal can give. We don't need to use them as often as we naturally do! If you can't give a clear and concise musical reason for why you just used your Crash cymbal, that means it was done out of habit rather than intent.

A great way of minimising your Crashes, while also thinking musically, is to only Crash when going into a dynamically larger section. So coming from a loud chorus into a quiet verse won't need one. Some of the most tasteful drumming I have seen has involved the drummer not touching a Crash cymbal until the penultimate moment of the song (usually the bridge or last chorus), so when they do finally land on the cymbal it has so much impact that it takes the song to a whole other level. The less you use it, the more impact it will have when you do.

VOICING OUR DRUM FILLS

This is a subject that gets asked a lot and surrounds the idea of where on the kit we play our drum fills. A drum kit has so many different 'voices' that choosing which ones to use in our fills can be a really tricky game. The first question to always ask is, 'Is a Drum Fill even needed?' A question that drummers rarely ask themselves...

Here is an interesting experience to have in your practice time that also emphasises this point; Put on 'Billie Jean' by Michael Jackson and play along to the entire song without playing a single drum fill, only the simple drum beat. Fairly soon you will begin to have a 'drummer itch' where you will want to add a drum fill, and eventually it will feel like you need to! It is in our physique to use drum fills, but it is a habit and a default reaction when we play that isn't always needed. The more fills we add as drummers, the less impact they will have. So first and foremost, always be asking what you are wanting that drum fill to achieve? What musical statement are you trying to make? A drum fill is primarily there to musically lead one section into another section, but again, only if really needed. So if you have made the decision to use a drum fill, how do we know what kind of fill to use?

It comes down to two things; Rate and Frequency/Tone. We play an instrument that covers pretty much the whole frequency range, cymbals being high, Snare and Small Toms sitting in the middle and large drums covering the low end. Being aware of this when we choose to play drum fills can dictate whether what we play is musically appropriate. It comes down to a simple equation; Which section of the song are we in, and which frequency would match this? If we are in a verse then a drum fill using all the Big Toms and Bass Drum would be super intrusive! Similarly, if we are using a drum fill to enter a huge chorus, then using the Hi-hat and Small Tom won't carry enough power. Knowing why the drum fill is being used, which section you are leading into and which tone is needed from your fills is the mindset needed for creating a musically wise drum fill! The 'Rate' is essentially how many notes you fit into your drum fill or how fast/slow it is.

We will cover this in more detail in the following point.
Keeping these factors in mind is what can take our drumming to a whole other level! This is because it passes just simply learning a number of set drum fills and then trying to 'shoe-horn' them into every song.

USING RATES OF NOTES (SUBDIVISION)

'Subdivision' or the 'Rate of notes': If those terms are unfamiliar, it is basically how fast or slow you are playing. Or more specifically, it is how many notes you are squeezing into one beat. A good understanding of this is the foundation for everything we do as drummers!

If the following paragraphs confuse you then it is really advisable to book a lesson with a local drum teacher and ask to cover the basic subdivisions. You're playing and musicianship will be eternally grateful!

So here are the basic 4 Subdivisions that we will be looking at, in a table that shows how they fit together within a beat:

1/4 Notes	1			2			3			4		
8th Notes	1		+	2		+	3		+	4		+
Triplets	1	Trip	Let	2	Trip	Let	3	Trip	Let	4	Trip	Let
16th Notes	1	e	+	a	2	e	+	a	3	e	+	a	4	e	+	a

SUBDIVISIONS WITHIN A GROOVE

When playing a standard drum groove, using different subdivisions on the Hi-hat can drastically change the entire feel and energy! 1/4 notes have a lot of space, 8th notes have less space and 16th notes have even less; this is exactly how it sounds when we use these subdivisions in a groove. It is a great way of changing the feel, without changing the main groove (the Kick and Snare pattern).

If you want to add lots of energy then try using 16th notes on a tightly closed Hi-hat, if you want to add power and space then try using 1/4 notes on an open Hi-hat. Exploring your creativity by being able to switch between these subdivisions can be an invaluable tool for giving your Worship Leader the 'feel' that they are after in a song.

SUBDIVISIONS WITHIN DRUM FILLS

This is an approach that can take a drummer's playing to another level when it is practiced and explored; using a variety of subdivisions within you drum fills. The natural habit is to stick to one rate of notes when we play a fill. Or at a push we will switch between 8th notes and 16th notes, which feels safe because they are multiples of 4 so divide evenly into each other. Using different subdivisions within one drum fill can have real power to add excitement, relaxation, or weight to a song.

View it as if you were a passenger on the motorway; if the driver suddenly starts speeding up then you immediately feel tense/excited. If the driver suddenly slows the car down then you prepare yourself for there to be less noise, movement, and progress. It is the same with drum fills! Depending where in the fill you start adding more notes can dictate where your band and congregation will think the song is heading.

And just a general tip; if you want a drum fill to sound huge, powerful, epic, and exciting then use triplets on beats 3 & 4. It is a subdivision that is so under-used but can sound great. But it is tricky cleanly switching from multiples of 4 to a triplet so practice, practice, practice!

'KEEPING TIME' USING SUBDIVISIONS

When playing in Churches, this point can be one of the most useful and valuable skills to learn. There will be many moments within a worship set where your job as the drummer is to simply "Keep Time". This essentially means when you are not playing a groove or particularly interesting rhythm, you are just using something (usually the Ride Cymbal or HiHats) to keep the rest of the band together during a quiet section.

Choosing which subdivision to use can have a real impact on where the band will feel like the song is going and how easy it is to stay with you. Here is a really simple yet golden technique; The more notes you add, the more tension and excitement will be felt.

If you are keeping time in a quiet section of a song, but you know that a big chorus is coming up, then use Subdivisions to make the band aware and transition them into a chorus smoothly. Start by keeping time on the Ride cymbal using 1/4 notes, as you get closer to the big chorus start using 8th notes, and the bar before the big fill use 16th notes! By doing this you are making it clear that there is a dynamic change coming, and also avoiding the sudden shock of a big drum fill that seems to come out of nowhere!

Choose wisely which subdivision you use when you are keeping time for a long duration. You want enough notes to keep the band together without being too busy or obvious, and this is unfortunately subjective to the feel, tempo, and dynamic of a specific song.

6 ESSENTIAL DRUM GROOVES

When you are a musician that has put years of time into bettering your skills and expanding your musical vocabulary, then the natural result is you end up with a seemingly endless pool of drum patterns and ideas. Although, the reality for a large number of churches is that their drummers just simply have not had that level of practice or training! So many drummers have started learning specifically to serve their church, others are drummers who play as a hobby, whilst others play another instrument and are trying their hand at the drums.

It is foolish to assume that everyone who sits behind a kit is a seasoned professional with years of experience and knowledge. But that still does not mean they cannot contribute and enhance their churches worship!

To help with this potential situation, here is a freebie that can be gold! Below, you will find 6 essential drum grooves that always pop up in church music! If you can become comfortable playing these 6 drum beats then it will definitely lower the chances of you having absolutely no idea what to play in church.

This is the starting point though, the practice material within this is to become accustomed with each groove and also work on variations of them. Try playing them slightly differently, at different speeds, using different subdivisions or adding/subtracting certain notes. THIS is how you expand your musical vocabulary as a drummer. GO PRACTICE!

KEY:

Bass · Snare · Small Tom · Middle Tom · Floor Tom · Hi-Hat · Crash · Ride

1. THE BASIC GROOVE

The foundation! This is the first and most important groove you should ever learn! You can get paid gigs if you can nail this groove. The Kick and Snare parts stay the same, but here we have three variations of each groove as your right hand is being played on a different drum/cymbal.

2. FOUR-ON-THE-FLOOR

If you can master this groove and get it feeling great, not only will your churches thank you but you can probably get some paid function work out of it. This is a groove that comes up all the time because it feels great and everyone can jump on top of it easily! One variation is to use 8th notes on the Hi-hat, and then start accenting the off beats (+'s) to get a funky/disco feel.

3. THE 6/8 GROOVE

This groove can frequently throw drummers off if you are not familiar or comfortable with it. Within church music, if you ever hear a song that sounds like it's not quite in 4/4 time then it is most likely in 6/8 time (The church hasn't gone to progressive yet with using odd time signatures). To put it into understandable terms, you essentially play 8th notes but you count them in 6's. Beats 1 and 4 are what we now use as the 'downbeat'.

Listen to these songs to hear how 6/8 time feels and sounds then practice playing along with them:
David Crowder: Come as you are
Housefires: Good Good Father

Some songs are in 3/4, which if we think mathematically should sound the same as it's the same number of notes. But actually, the main difference is the **feel** of both grooves. The general idea is that to play in 6/8 means the backbeat is on '4' and the groove has some 'bounce' to it. 3/4 is much straighter and the backbeat is usually on '3'. It all comes down to feel!

One great example is found on one album; listen to Chris Sayburn's tracks 'Nothing but Grace' (3/4) and 'Great is the Lord' (6/8) and hear the difference between both tracks. If it's confusing then its good to get a lesson with a teacher to explain it fully!

4. BIG TOM GROOVE

This groove is a gold mine for drummers and is a regularly requested groove. Sometimes a full drum beat is way too much and isn't needed in a song, but the worship leader still needs something rhythmic! Playing a rolling rhythm on a Big Tom can work wonders in keeping some time and also some interest. The main thing when playing a groove on the Tom is to think about the accents, and that is where the variations start happening. Practice coming up with different accents over the 16th notes.

Keep the sticking the same (R L R L ...) and practice accenting different notes and hearing what you come up with! You can even try moving the accents to a different tom to create some melody in your groove. Also, try adding a Snare on beat 4 to add some interest and more of a groove if needed. Have fun with this one!

5. STRAIGHT KICK AND CYMBAL

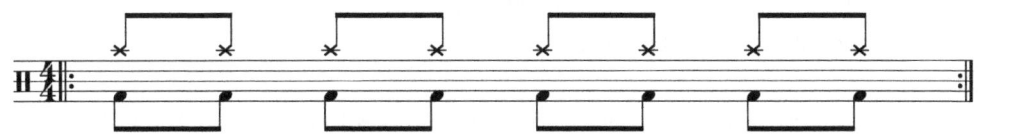

Dead easy but so useful! This can work great for either a build or a groove. Sometimes when you hit the penultimate section of a song where you need as much power as you can, this groove is perfect! This is because it is powerful, simple, and has space.

Put both your hands on some cymbals (Crashes or open Hi-hats), choose a subdivision and start pulsing. This works for keeping time and also gives the other instruments space to create a huge sound! It works really well in Bridges and Instrumentals when you need some serious power, without it sounding messy.

6. DISPLACED SNARE DRUM

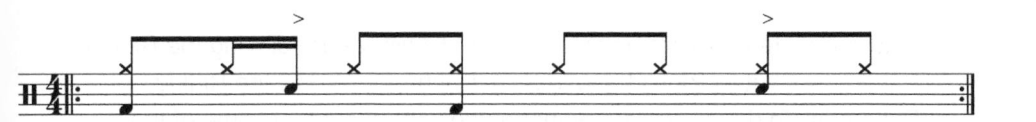

Again, this groove is the initial idea but needs to be practiced in order to come up with some variations. The idea of a 'displaced' groove is that the Snare doesn't simply land on 2 and 4. Because of this, it gives it an interesting and spacious feel which is so useful in church music.

Practice taking the Snare that is usually on beat 2 or 4 and moving it to a different point in the beat. Off-beat 16th notes ('e' and 'a') sound great!

CHANGING THE FEEL, NOT THE GROOVE

These ideas perfectly follow the 6 Essential Grooves, and they show a way of completely changing the feel of a groove without actually changing the groove! Deep stuff...

This concept is invaluable for making a song breathe and grow, without having to spend a lifetime learning every groove and pattern under the sun. When we look at how a drum groove is constructed, we usually see a Kick Pattern (Bass Drum), a Backbeat (Snare Drum) and a Riding Pattern (Hihat or Ride Cymbal). These three components together are what give us the basic drum grooves that we know so well and are familiar with. When we look deeper into what the role of each component is, we can see why some grooves work better than others in certain songs.

As a general rule, the Kick Pattern and Backbeat are what the rest of the band will rely on and these are essentially the main components of our drum grooves. Sometimes, it is wise not to change these key elements if they are working perfectly with the song. In order to change the feel of a groove (without changing the key elements), we need to turn to the last component, the Riding Pattern.

This is the idea; We are going to change HOW we are playing the Riding Pattern, so that we don't have to actually change WHAT the Riding Pattern is. To do this we are going to use something that some of the world's best drummers utilise beautifully in their playing; ACCENTS. To recap, an Accent is essentially a louder stroke in comparison to the rest of the notes. When we use Accents in our Riding Patterns we can completely change the feel of a drum groove.

We are going to look at a few of the simplest ideas to really show just how useful this idea is. Let's take a drum groove which we usually learn from day one of drumming. However, we are going to look at 5 different

Riding Patterns and how they change the overall sound and feel of that groove. By using a variety of Riding Patterns for different sections of a song, you can increase or decrease the intensity and dynamic, without actually changing the groove that you are playing. This idea is gold for both the beginner and experienced drummers out there!

Here are the 5 variations:

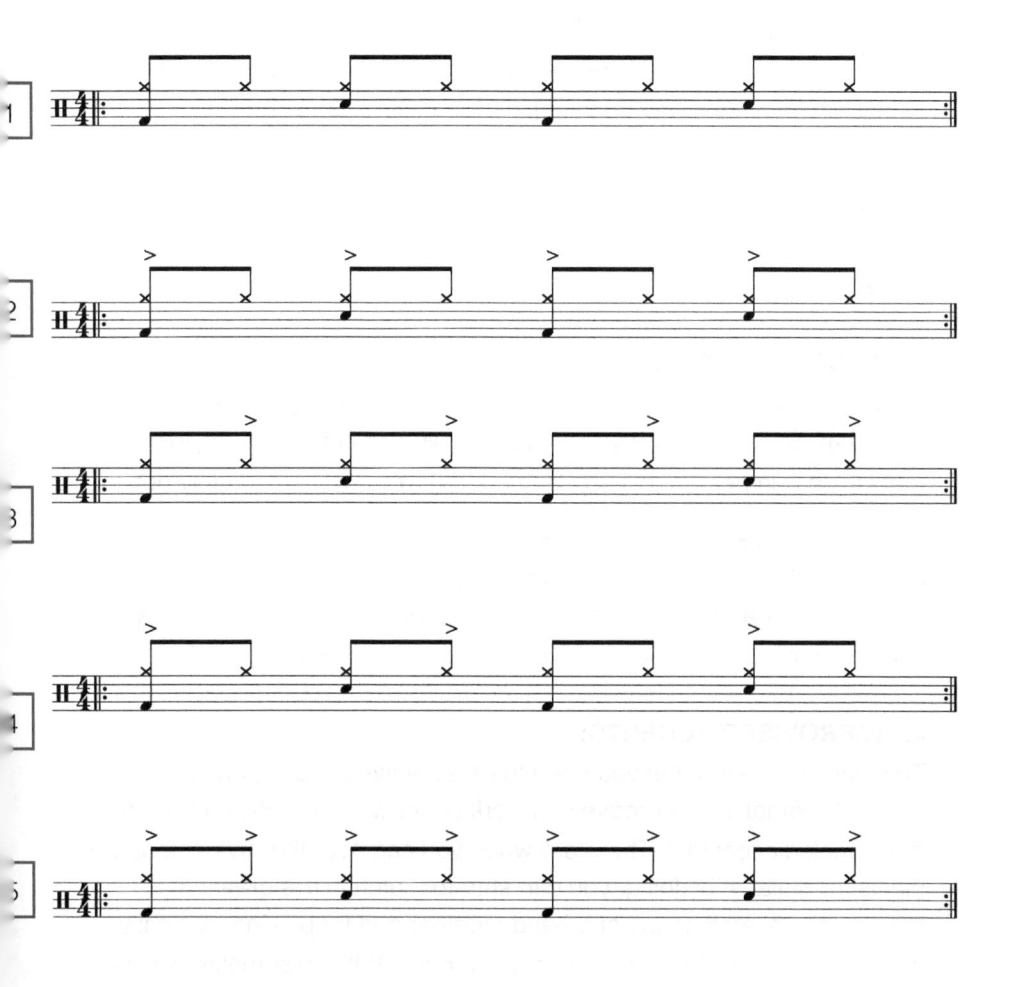

1. ALL UN-ACCENTED:

This is where it all begins; every note is equal volume and is unaccented (quiet). Straight away you will notice how much more your Bass and Snare Drum stand out when you reduce the volume of your cymbals. This will give a punchier and bolder drum groove as the lower frequencies will appear to be boosted becasue you are reducing the higher frequencies from the cymbals.

2. ACCENTED DOWN-BEATS:

This groove has all the down-beats accented! So if you were counting along, all the numbers will be louder (① + ② + ③ + ④ +).

This gives a much more solid sound sound to your groove and will increase intensity as it sounds like you are starting to build into something. This is great to do a bar before you land into a bigger section of a song.

3. ACCENTED OFF-BEATS:

This is the opposite of number 2 and involves accenting all the off-beats in the bar. So, if you were counting along, you would accent anything that isn't a number (1 ⊕ 2 ⊕ 3 ⊕ 4 ⊕). You will immediately notice

that your groove now has more energy and excitement to it. You are essentially filling in the gaps between the Bass and Snare drum so it sounds busier and as though there is more going on. Great if you want to give the song some busy-ness, liveliness, and excitement.

4. IMPROVISED ACCENTS:

This one can be fun, but you need to be selective about when and how to use it. Sometimes a groove can work better when the Riding Pattern has a melodic feel to it. Therefore when you can hear the rhythm that the pianist or guitarist is doing, you can start to match it. It is great for bringing the overall sound of a band together and for playing musically over your groove. But be careful not to overdo it! It can sometimes sound messy and erratic if done in the wrong places.

5. ALL ACCENTED:

The final accent option is to accent the whole Riding Pattern. This will sound larger, more powerful, and have more weight to your groove. Great to use in a Chorus or Bridge where you need a larger dynamic. When you switch between accenting none of the notes, to accenting all of them, you will really notice the difference in sound and feel.

By using this mindset when playing any groove, you will be amazed at how you can completely change the feel and dynamic of a consistent, repeating drum beat. One of the biggest irritations found in Bass players is that the drummer isn't keeping a consistent pattern to lock onto.

The reason drummers don't keep a consistent pattern is because they are trying to build dynamics by changing the WHOLE groove. We honestly don't need to! We can just change how we are accenting the Riding Pattern and still get through a whole song, making it musically and dynamically interesting.

A great exercise is to try and play a whole song with no fills at all, only changing the Riding Pattern accents to see if you can still make a song breathe. A quick example would be to play Riding Pattern 1 in a verse, pattern 2 as a fill and then pattern 5 in the chorus.

It can genuinely work and also means you will never be accused of 'over-playing'.

THE EXAMPLE

Thinking about all of the above is what can separate the amateur drummer from the musical drummer. Think about the sound your instrument is making and the vast number of options available to you, and it can become easy to play a whole song without using a single drum fill.

Bearing in mind everything we have just read, here is an example of playing minimally, yet dynamically throughout an imaginary song. It is all groove based, only using a Flam as a fill (sparingly), and focusing on HOW we are playing not WHAT we are playing.

Here is a really simple guide to making a song flow with dynamics whilst also playing the absolute minimum:

SECTION	DYNAMIC	DRUMMING
INTRO	POWERFUL	Click in, Big solid groove on an open Hi-Hat, using the shoulder of the stick
BAR BEFORE VERSE		Build on the floor tom
VERSE	QUIET BUT STILL PLAYING	Closed Hi-hat, tip of the stick on the top of the cymbal, strong kick but no rimshot on the snare, play in the middle of the drum head with the tip of the stick.
BAR BEFORE CHORUS		Start using the Shoulder of the stick and gently opening the Hi-hat.
CHORUS	ALL OUT	Big Crash on 1, then keep time on the Ride cymbal with the tip of the stick.

BAR BEFORE LINK	ALL OUT	Double the subdivision to indicate a section change is coming, maybe even start gently crashing on the Ride.
LINK	POWERFUL	Strong groove, open Hi-hat, use rim-shots on the snare.
BAR BEFORE VERSE		Flam on beat 4.
VERSE	SOLID	A solid groove, but no rim-shot and use the tip of the stick on top of a closed Hi-hat.
BAR BEFORE CHORUS		Start using the shoulder of the stick on the Hi-hat and opening the cymbals slightly.
CHORUS	POWERFUL	Full groove, play on the Ride Cymbal and use Rim-shots on the Snare.
BAR BEFORE BRIDGE		Keep the groove, but drop out the Snare Drum
BRIDGE X2	1ST TIME: OUT 2ND TIME: BIG	1st: Keep time on the Ride Cymbal 2nd: Start adding Kick Drums or use a full groove.
BAR BEFORE CHORUS		Double the subdivision on the cymbals and use a flam on the last beat.
CHORUS	POWERFUL	Full and present drum groove, use the Ride cymbal. Use rim-shots!
BAR BEFORE OUTRO		Flam on the last beat.
OUTRO	VERY BIG!!	Full groove

WHEN STUFF GOES WRONG

To put this plainly, we are musicians and we are also human. This inevitably means that mistakes can sometimes happen. Some of the best learning moments come from making a mistake and analysing why it happened, how to avoid it in future, and how it could have been resolved quicker.

One of the main qualities that separate the professionals from the beginners is obviously how frequently mistakes are made, but more importantly how well mistakes are covered up when they do happen.

It is hilarious when a great musician lists the mistakes that were made during a set that no one even noticed because they covered it up like a champ! Here are just a few ideas that can help with this, which can make your music team work better together and also keep yourself as a drummer solid and dependable.

OUR NEW DEFAULT REACTION; SEIZE AND ADJUST

SEIZE; *to take hold suddenly and forcibly.*
ADJUST; *Alter or move (something) in order to achieve a desired fit, appearance or result.*

THIS needs to become our default reaction as drummers when faced with a problem. The term 'forcibly' is usually used in a negative light, but in this situation it essentially refers to taking the reins of a problem and moving everything back to where it should be. When something goes wrong on stage there are usually two reactions; everyone flounders and looks for direction from anywhere, or someone immediately takes charge and gets everything back on track. Sometimes as drummers that second scenario falls to us because we are the rock and foundation for everything that is happening on stage.

How we play can usually aid and help our musicians and get them all back on the same page. So, it is a case of noticing that stuff is falling apart, getting eye contact and bringing people back on the right path. This might mean obvious drum fills, mouthing the lyrics so people know where they are in the song, or using Crash cymbals obviously on beat 1 of every bar to bring people back onto the right beat.

Mistakes are always subjective and unique, so it is a case of being aware of what is going on and becoming an anchor for the other musicians to use to ground themselves.

AVOID ANY 'EXPLOSION OR HANDBRAKE' MOMENTS

Even within our day to day living, one of the most natural reactions when faced with something going wrong is to immediately distance ourselves. When something isn't working (and it is obvious) it can be a really intimidating and scary moment when you have no idea what's happened or how you can fix it. In a musical sense, this can lead to what I call an 'Explosion or Handbrake' moment. The character of an explosion is that it goes from being calm and still, to startlingly loud within a single blink! On the other hand, a handbrake takes a situation that has momentum and movement, and suddenly grinds it to an immediate stop. This is usually quite uncomfortable.

If we transfer these pictures into a musical setting, we have two very common, but unpleasant sounds. Here is an example; let us imagine that we are not playing anything, but it turns out the worship leader expected us to bring a groove into that section. Having realised we missed a cue, we panic and suddenly start playing a full groove. The problem with this is that we have already missed beat one, so to suddenly start playing a groove can sound explosive and erratic! On the flip side, we might be playing a groove and the worship leader didn't actually want us to. To suddenly stop playing can sound awkward and uncomfortable...

Part of our job as a whole worship team is to take our congregation on a worship-filled journey, and part of that role is not to create an environment that is distracting. If you missed a cue to start playing (for any number of reasons, sometimes not even your fault), don't crash into a groove a bar late to try and recover. It will sound inappropriate and highlight that you clearly missed a signal. If you are playing a groove and the leader signals that you shouldn't be doing that, don't just stop drumming in the middle of a bar! The best tactic for this is to give a big nod to your worship leader so they know you understand and then begin changing your playing so that you can smoothly and musically reach the desired dynamic. The following point is a great way of doing this;

THE FADE IN/OUT TECHNIQUE

This technique is gold and can make mistakes appear non-existent to a congregation. It most commonly happens when a signal has been misread, misgiven, or just not seen at all. Usually it is about whether the next section is going to be loud or quiet, or whether your worship leader would like drums to come in.

Let's say a signal has been read as "I would like the drums to start a groove", so you start playing, only to then be immediately shushed and waved down; this is where it can get really awkward. The natural reaction here is to immediately stop what you're doing, and this is normal and what is expected. But let's think about how this can sound to a congregation.

Picture this scenario; you are the passenger in a car and you are dozing off to sleep while your friend drives. As you fall asleep, the car in front suddenly brakes. If your friend also slams on their brakes, you would wake up startled and know something was wrong! If your friend reacted quickly by calmly driving around the car in front, then the chances are you wouldn't even wake up. The same problem happened in both scenarios, but the driver's reaction dictated the passengers reaction.

This can be similar when we play drums and misread a signal or when no signal was given at all. If we start playing and it has become clear that it is not what the Worship Leader wanted, to just stop playing can highlight that a mistake has clearly happened. Whereas, calmly reducing what we are playing to fade it out calmly can sound like a deliberate musical decision.

The best way to fade out isn't to reduce the volume of the whole groove. It is actually better to remove certain elements of the groove until nothing is left. If you are playing a full groove, start by playing the Snare drum only on beat 4, then remove the Snare drum completely. Then only use your bass drum and reduce the number of notes you are playing until you are left with just a cymbal. Then reduce how many notes you are playing on the cymbal. If done well, you can fade out a groove within 4 bars which will sound like a deliberate musical decision, not a mistake that you 'hand-braked' to a halt!

If the opposite has happened and you should be playing but are not, then use the same technique but start from the other end. Bring a cymbal in, then some bass drum, then your snare, then the full groove.

WORST COMES TO WORST; KEEP TIME

As drummers, one of our main jobs is to keep the rest of the musicians on the same page and give them a foundation to work with. When a musical situation hits a bump and people are struggling to make head or tail of it, it can sometimes be better to just keep a sense of pulse so that everyone knows where beat 1 is. Giving your musicians a strong indicator of where the pulse is, and where the core beats are, gives them an anchor to grab onto and steady themselves. This can be done on a cymbal or a bass drum.

The main trick is to accent beat 1 to make it obvious where it is!

This can also sometimes involve listening to what the worship leader is doing and bringing the rest of the band back onto their track. Keeping time is an invaluable tool and can usually work a lot better than a full drum beat, as that can just sound messy and confusing if the rest of the band aren't sure what's going on.

Number one tip; STAY CALM. Panic is contagious, pointing blame is unhelpful, and distancing yourself from the problem leaves everyone else stranded.

READY, SET, WORSHIP!

This section is so crucial; never forget why you are there. Worship is a huge component of church life and is not to be taken half-heartily. So much of the content written in this book focuses heavily on the practical and logistical problems and solutions, but at the end of the day you are there to bring people into a worshipful place and 'logistics' will only be so important. So stay observant of the congregation and the general atmosphere of the room. The following points are how you can stay aware and reactive to the atmosphere/response happening in the room, and also worship through what you are doing.

ALWAYS KEEP YOUR HEAD UP (Literally)

Visually observing what is happening around you is a sure way of not missing something important. You need to be looking for cues, signals, musical changes, technical problems, congregational reactions, and overall responsiveness. You are there to help people worship so always be aware and watchful for what is happening in the room and on stage. Being drummers, this is sadly where we make a big sacrifice in worship; due to logistics and practicalities we have to be conscious of when we worship and be wise in that choice.

Closing your eyes is a great way of blocking out the outside world, but it does exactly that! Having your eyes open is how you will see signals and cues so when we close our eyes it has to be in a moment when we are confident that nothing is going to be changing. It can sound like an obvious point, but it can be so awkward when a band is needing to musically move somewhere but the drummer is lost in their own world. It can be bittersweet...

ALWAYS BE THINKING AHEAD

You can only do this to a certain degree due to the fact you are not the worship leader. By having a general idea/feeling of where you think the song is going to go and the atmosphere you want to create can help with transitioning smoothly into different sections. If you only think about what you are playing as you are playing it then making any dynamic/musical change can become 'clunky' and sound like a mistake, which in turn becomes distracting; the exact opposite of what we want as worship drummers...

UNLIKE THE 10 COMMANDMENTS, A CHURCH SET LIST IS RARELY SET IN STONE

A quick disclaimer; this applies more to churches who a building a culture of sponatoues worship. The general format found is that at the start of each service you will be given a set list with a number of songs on it. You will then rehearse said songs with the aim to play them in the service when directed to do so. This sounds like an organised and stress-free system for conducting a music team! If only this were true...

There is a strong chance that this setlist will change! Occasionally (if lucky) it will be after a quick briefing before you walk on stage, but it is not uncommon for the Worship Leader to simply start playing a song you may have never even heard of. The reason this can be a common occurrence is because we are not doing a gig or prewritten concert, we are playing in an atmosphere that should be primarily Spirit-Lead. So if your Worship Leader is feeling called to play a certain song and is responding to that call, then it is your job as their drummer to get on board asap!

Reacting in the moment is a skill that can only really be learnt while being forced to do it, and churches naturally give you that experience. In some cases it can even be just a single look from the band leader, who will mouth the name of a song and then wait for you to count in! Your choices here are either play something, or just stare at the bass player and stop the whole service.

COMMUNICATION: HINTING

This is an idea that is invaluable for understanding your Worship Leader and where they want a song to go. We read in the first chapter how at its very core, the drums are a communication instrument. That was one of the initial purposes, to convey messages over distances and send warnings or information. Even today (with our modern drum sets) we can still have this attitude, which in turn can completely change how we approach our playing. The idea of 'Hinting' is essentially testing the water for what your worship leader wants. It is a way of subtly asking a question and then gauging your playing on the response. Communication at its finest!

The definition of a 'hint' is, *a slight or indirect indication or suggestion.* So, it is a way of making a small suggestion and seeing if your worship leader agrees or not. How does this practically look on a drum kit? It comes down to introducing elements of your idea instead of playing the whole thing. Let's use an example that is very common. We are playing a song and the dynamic is very low and quiet, so as drummers we are currently not playing. We feel that the dynamic needs to grow and a drum groove needs to start being used. The usual options here are to either start playing a groove without being given a signal, or to sit and wait for a signal. This can be frustrating when we have a feeling that the song needs to move, and no signal is coming. However, if we just start playing, it could sound hideously inappropriate.

There is a third option though, which surrounds the idea of 'hinting'. In order to hint to a worship leader about an idea, you need to start INTRODUCING elements of the idea. So, if you are coming up to a new section and feel that it needs to start lifting, you could start introducing the Ride cymbal. This shows you feel the song needs to be moving forward and growing dynamically. If you feel it needs to grow even more, then start introducing a bass drum to hint that you want to add a groove. If the worship leader doesn't say otherwise and even starts joining you, that is your green light. If you get the 'don't-play-please' wave, then all you do is stop playing the bass drum.

The reason that hinting works so well is because it is easier and less obvious to introduce elements of an idea, and then bring them back out if the Worship Leader doesn't think it's the right decision. If you bring in a full drum beat and are then told not to do it, it is so much more obvious if you just stop playing it because you have already started using the whole idea. Whereas, bringing in some Ride cymbal and bass drum can subtly be silenced without drawing too much attention from the congregation. Great ways of hinting towards an idea are by adding or subtracting elements of what you are playing!

If you feel a song needs to dynamically grow, try adding some more cymbals and bass drum. If you feel a song needs to become dynamically quieter, try dropping out the snare drum to hint that you are bringing the groove out. It is a case of not making sudden or extreme decisions. Make a hint towards what you are thinking of doing before you actually have to, which is essentially asking whether your worship leader agrees with you. If the worship leader's playing starts to reflect what you are thinking, that is a big Go sign to do what you think needs to happen.

ENJOY IT AND WORSHIP THROUGH IT

Drums were invented initially to be a communicative instrument and have been used throughout history to convey messages, warnings, and excitement. It therefore seems illogical to not have that mindset whilst we ourselves are playing that instrument. Remember that you are playing the drums as a sign of your own personal worship!

So choose to worship God through your playing and it can take you into a whole other headspace, which is an incredible feeling! To reiterate; **Great skill without a worshipful heart to lead it just creates a musically impressive gig, leaving no room for the spirit to work or for God to be glorified.**

*

"A FIELD MANUAL;
BECAUSE IT NEEDS TO BE TAKEN INTO THE FIELD"

"As the drummer it is your job to keep everything together and be the foundation that the rest of the band can build on so knowing what you are working with really helps."

SIX
THE INVITATION

THE FIELD MANUAL

6

THE INVITATION
HOW TO APPROACH BEING INVOLVED IN AN UNFAMILIAR CHURCH

This chapter can easily be applied to all playing situations that you may find yourself in, but we are going to specifically dive into what it looks like to drum at a church that you are unfamiliar with. Much like session musicians and bands working within a musical circuit, worship leaders and band members seem to regularly become acquainted with one another. If a situation has arisen where a worship leader has found themselves 'drummer-less' for a service, then the natural solution is to ring around other church drummers that they know and see who is free and willing.

So an invitation to play in a different church can come from a variety of places; an email or a phone call from a worship pastor, a friend of a friend, the sister of your friend's girlfriends dad, etc… The invitation could come from any church with varying traditions, music teams, congregations, and buildings. Although the style of church may be different, in this situation they are all valid and all have one thing in common; they need a drummer.

This chapter basically gives a simple overview of how to approach the initial invitation, through to arriving at the church itself. There are certain approaches that we can take as drummers to ensure that an unfamiliar church still gets the best from us, and a large majority of this comes from how much prep we do.

THE INTIAL CONTACT

As we read before, the initial contact can come from anywhere and from anyone. But there will always be the same information needed in order to gauge your approach for how to give that church your best. The more information you can find out before you get there the better! The obvious questions are where the church is and what songs they are expecting to do. However, there are some slightly more abstract questions that can also help you prep.

Some useful info to find out:
Will there be a drum kit provided? (never assume there will be...)
Does that Church use Fold-Backs/Stage Monitors, In-Ear Monitors or nothing?
Do they want a mid-week practice, or do they practice before the service?
How big is the room/Is there a Screen around the kit?
Who else is in the band? (You may know some of the other musicians involved!).

All of these details are useful for being prepared, but there are also some more aspects to keep in mind. Here are a few points to consider which will hopefully aid you in playing at an unfamiliar church:

THERE IS NO TIME FOR 'PLAYING HARD TO GET'

Modern technology has created a social culture of 'immediate response'. This is a blessing when needing to find information quickly, but is also a burden regarding our patience for when we expect that information. Obviously, life as a musician can be hectic, but the speediness in responding to messages or emails can dictate the happiness of anybody who is asking for your help. It is never fun being sent the 'just-checking-you-got-my-last-email' message...

Being honourable, humble and servant-hearted starts from the second you receive a call, and how you respond to that invitation. If you can make the event then let your contact know as soon as you can, and if you can't make the event then also let your contact know as soon as you can.

SETTING OFF

HAVING 'GOOD TIMING' GOES BEYOND PLAYING THE DRUMS

This point was made in a previous chapter, but is so important that it is being repeated in this section. I have heard of more musicians never being called back for more work simply on the basis that they turned up after the requested arrival time, or were even late getting on stage when they were actually in the venue! Nothing causes more tension than waiting for one person so that you can all start setting up/sound checking/leading worship. If you want to give your best and serve a church that is musically in need, then don't ever be that drummer who keeps people waiting…

PREPARE FOR THE WORST

There is an attitude I have when playing at an unfamiliar church, which may sound negative but it is actually a way of guaranteeing that that church gets the best from me; **Expect and Prepare for the worst**. This is not implying that you have to enter a new church expecting it to be the worst musical experience of your life, but this point comes down to one key thing: Equipment. A lot of churches are not granted a budget that stretches far enough to buy top end music equipment and drum kits. This is out of your control, but there are a few things you can take with you that can cover a multitude of problems. And here they are:

WHAT TO KEEP IN THE BOOT OF YOUR CAR

YOUR NICE SNARE DRUM & CYMBALS
A nice Snare Drum and some decent cymbals can completely lift the sound of a drum kit! If the Toms sound completely hideous then you can just avoid playing them. If you can get a great Snare and cymbal set onto an average sounding kit, it is amazing how much difference that makes. On a psychological level, you will also be playing elements of the kit that you are now familiar with which can create a sense of trust and confidence in the gear you are using. This will naturally lead to your drumming feeling more comfortable and your mind being free to focus on what you are playing, not how the gear sounds.

YOUR DRUM STOOL
I have lost count of the number of churches I have played at where the drum stool is set to a single height, and it is always as low as it can go… Have one with you as a back up to be on the safe side. It could be argued that one of the most terrifying experiences that a drummer can go through is when a drum stool randomly drops from beneath you! Avoid this genuine fear of death by keeping your stool in the boot of your car, just incase you simply don't trust the stool that is there.

A USABLE KICK PEDAL
A decent kick pedal can work wonders on a 'not-so-great' Kick Drum. If you end up having to play a whole service on a pedal that wont move unless you put your whole body weight behind it then that's no fun at all… No one likes hearing a loud squeak every time your foot moves, and it's even less enjoyable for you if you can't play as musically as you would like due to the pedal not working with you. Have one in your car just incase the pedal on their kit is becoming a hindrance and you need to quickly and subtly switch them over.

WHAT TO KEEP IN YOUR POCKETS AND STICK BAG

YOUR DRUMSTICKS
It's obvious, but can happen… Never forget sticks because it's super embarrassing and difficult to rectify.

MOON GEL/DAMPENERS
One thing that seems to be commonly neglected on church drum kits is the frequency of 'Head Changes'. The drum head is one of the key factors to whether a drum kit sounds any good, and yet some kits will have had the same heads on for decades. Now tuning the kit can obviously change the tone, pitch and overall sound of a kit, but if you don't have time then cover it in dampeners!

Dampening can remove a lot of unwanted and unforgivably hideous overtones. Dampening pads (Moon-gel, Slapklatz or Drum-Dots, to name a few brands) are affordable and kill a lot of overtones without losing the core tone of the drum. Throwing these onto the heads of a pretty beat up kit can completely change the amount of 'nastiness' that will come from the drums.

DRUM KEY
As a good habit, buy a drum key and just carry it on your key chain so that you always have one to hand. These little keys are the universal tool that tighten and loosen practically every lug or screw on a drum kit. Pretty much every drum brand creates their hardware to be compatible with a standard drum key, so they are invaluable to carry with you when you are playing on a kit that isn't your own.

If you have time (and permission) to tune the kit a little then it is impossible without a drum key. Some churches will be more than happy for a drummer to come in and tune their drum kit, while others will look at you like you are vandalising their drum kit.

So always ask before you start turning any lugs! If the church is happy for you to tune up the heads then work your magic to get the kit sounding just that little bit sweeter. Having a drum key on your person at all times is a good habit to get into so that as and when something just doesn't sound right, you have the tools to fix it pretty quickly.

IN-EAR HEADPHONES AND EAR PLUGS
A lot of churches are moving to in-ear monitoring instead of on stage monitors (Fold-Backs or Wedges), so always keep a pair of in-ears with you just in case. If this church uses fold-backs then also have ear plugs with you so that you can protect your ears while also being able to hear what you need to.

Noise cancelling in-ears are the best choice; please never use anything like iPod headphones! You'll need to have the volume so loud to be able to hear over the kit that there's more chance of rupturing an ear drum... Your hearing is your number one tool so look after it as if it was your child!

HEADPHONE ADAPTER (Small Jack to Big Jack)
Alongside the previous point, always have a jack adapter just incase you need to plug into a small mixer which only has a 1/4 inch jack output, which will be too big for a standard headphone jack to fit into. It saves you and the sound engineer a lot of time if you can fix these problems yourself.

For a bonus point, have a headphone extension cable on you as well in case the mixer is on the floor or miles away from where you are sat.

All of these items can save so much time and frustration when playing at a church you are unfamiliar with. If you can rectify small problems or irritations yourself then you will keep the Church, the worship team and the sound engineer happy.

PRE-SERVICE INTEL

This is essential for giving the best you can to a group of musicians, whilst also getting the best out of the whole team you are working with. The amount of 'Pre-Service Intel' you can collect will determine how you approach your own playing and the band dynamic as a whole. As the drummer, it is your job to keep everything together and be the foundation that the rest of the band can build on. Knowing what you are working with really helps.

MAKE FRIENDS WITH THE BAND EARLY

The Church is built on community; this applies even when you are at a new Church with unfamiliar faces. You are all there for one reason, which is to help a group of people meet with Jesus in a deeper way. If the team leading the worship are not on the same page then how can we expect to pick up a congregation and take them with us in worship? So these are important questions when arriving at a new church to gauge what you are working with: Who is this team of musicians? What do they do outside of church? Are they regular members of this church? Do they play their instrument outside of church? How friendly are they?

Music as a whole is used as a communicative, social, and spiritual tool, so become aware of who you are playing with and what the dynamic of the music team is. This will make it easier to find where your role fits in to this unfamiliar team.

LEARN THE SOUND ENGINEER'S NAME!

This can be so essential but also so easy to forget! The sound person is the one that makes everything happen and more importantly will be the one running to your aid if something goes wrong with your equipment. One key way to show respect and appreciation is by knowing someone's name, to avoid calling them 'mate' or 'sound guy' for the rest of the service. Always make friends with the 'Soundy' and honour them by communicating with them on a personal level.

WHO IS IN WHOSE EYE LINE?

This is a vital piece of information to figure out as quickly as possible! As soon as all the musicians are on the stage, observe who can see who. How many musicians can see the worship leader clearly? How many musicians can see you clearly? What percentage of the team can't you see? This gives you a clear insight into where to look for signals, who the natural leaders are when the band starts playing, and which musicians you will be able to communicate with while playing.

Eye contact can be everything when trying to communicate with other musicians. Being able to clearly see the individual who is leading the worship can lessen the likelihood of missing signals, cues, and musical directions. You are playing with a 'Musical Team' which will naturally require some teamwork and communication.

ABOVE ALL ELSE...

Above all else, enjoy yourself and worship through what you are doing. Churches are usually so grateful when a musician steps up and serves outside of their own familiar surroundings. Be friendly, be humble, be serving, and play your best. As drummers, it is about how we honour that Church, honour God, and honour ourselves.

"God is not unjust; he will not forget your work and the love you have shown him as you have helped his people and continue to help them."
(Hebrews 6:10 NIV)

*

"...WE ARE ALWAYS CALLED **TO GIVE OUR BEST** TO ANY OF THE CHURCHES **THAT WE FIND OURSELVES IN;** CONGREGATION SIZES AND THE STANDARD OF EQUIPMENT **DO NOT CHANGE THAT."**

SEVEN
THE INTIMATE CHURCH

7

THE INTIMATE CHURCH

PLAYING IN AN ENVIRONMENT WHERE ALL THE LIGHTS, AMPLIFIERS, AND MICROPHONES ARE NOT NEEDED

The previous chapters in this book were heavily focussed on the church services that require a full band with a full backline and PA. As fun as these services are to play, they are not the only setting that we can find ourselves in. It can be so easy to focus on the large church settings and give 100% in those situations, whilst potentially overlooking the intimate church setting.

Good musicianship and a worship-filled character is noticeable and valued in ALL styles of Church, and the opposite (poor musicianship and a worship-less character) cause problems in ALL styles of Church. It's about changing the musical mindset and practicalities, not the attitude.

Both are different environments, but both still carry great potential for worship. Our attitude towards this church setting shouldn't change at all, it is our musical approach that needs to be revisited. We read earlier how drums carry so much importance within music, which definitely translates into all environments.

As drummers, we are always called to give our best to any of the churches that we find ourselves in; congregation sizes and the standard of equipment do not change that. The Church is the Church.

THE DIFFERENCE IN EQUIPMENT & APPROACH

So practically, how can we adjust our playing to accommodate the musicians and congregation in these intimate church settings? Here are a few points to bear in mind:

It will come as no surprise that the equipment used in a small church will be very different to that of a mega church or large-scale building. There is no need for a 48-channel mixing desk and multiple sub-woofers in a room that holds 30 people. But just because the equipment is different in an intimate church, doesn't mean that we are destined to have a service where everything sounds terrible and we just stomach whatever noise comes out. We can still make our kit and drumming sound great to give the best we can to that church.

THE DRUM KIT

Step 1 is about the drum kit. What kit is best to use for these smaller church rooms and how can we get them sounding great? We live in an age where the variety of drum kits available is utterly overwhelming! For a start, there are so many different brands, with different kit sizes, made from different shell materials. Without going into comparing a multitude of different drum kits, there is a STYLE of kit that most brands will make that can work amazingly in the less-spacious church halls.

Search for either a Bop Kit, Jungle Kit, Jazz Kit or Compact Kit, and you can usually find a drum kit that has all the necessary components. However, the drum shell sizes are slightly smaller than your average drum kit. So, if we say that an average Bass Drum size is around 22 inches by 20 inches, then a compact kit might have a Bass Drum which is around 18"x16". The drum kit that I use for weddings and small church venues has a Bass Drum that is only 16"x16", which is the same size as the Big Tom on my main kit!

Now when we have a drum kit that has smaller shell dimensions than normal, it will take up less room and also be easier to move around, which is perfect! But what about the sound? Usually the smaller the drum the less depth and 'low end' is produced, which isn't too bad for small Toms. However, this can be a problem when wanting a deep Bass Drum sound, while only having the room for a compact Bass Drum. But there are ways around this; Tuning and Head selection. Here is one option in a quick nutshell; choose super thick heads and tune them pretty low. Add some dampening to eliminate any high-end ring, and you should be left with a deeper tone than usual. Look back through the 'In the Field' chapter to see the tuning options.

THE CYMBALS

Cymbals can be loud… It is a big lump of metal that we are hitting with a solid stick, so naturally this can create a loud noise. Now although it can be hard to find cymbals that are audibly quieter in volume (although some companies have now developed these), there is a certain type of cymbal we can use that reduces the amount of projection that the cymbal gives. Cymbals come in a variety of styles and are made in slightly different ways to give a certain sound. Lathed, hammered, natural, polished, brilliant, dark, dry, and brightness are all terms that you will find when browsing for cymbals. When playing in a small and intimate environment, there is a certain cymbal type that can make the world of difference; DRY CYMBALS.

For a cymbal to be 'dry' means that after you have struck it, the sustain of the cymbal dies off quicker. The dryer the cymbal, the less sustain it has. When playing in a small room, using a cymbal with a ton of sustain, brightness, and ring can be really hard to control and can overpower everything else. Using cymbals that have a dark tone and a lot of dryness can sit in the mix really nicely, be easier to control, and won't fill the whole room. The amount of dark and dry cymbals on the market is extraordinary, so if you start with those two terms then you are on the right path. Another little trick is to actually add dampening to your cymbals! This removes even more of that unwanted 'ringy-ness' and creates an even dryer sound.

DRUMMERS HATE/ARE UNABLE TO PLAY QUIETLY...

One of the main complaints directed at drummers from musicians and congregations is that they only have one dynamic volume; LOUD. Practicing to play quietly can be one of the most tedious, most difficult, yet most useful skill we can acquire as drummers. More often than not, we can find ourselves in musical situations where the venue is tiny, and the congregation is no more than a few feet away.

In a large venue, where the drum kit is behind a screen and has microphones all over it, the sound engineer has so much more control over the volume of our playing. If we are playing to loud, then they can just lower the mic gains. Whereas, playing in a small church with no microphones leaves us entirely in control of the volume of our playing, which gives us another aspect to be mentally aware of. As with anything regarding our drumming, shortcuts and tricks will only get us so far.

Spending the time to practice playing quietly is the only way to really get decent at it, but here are a few tips and tricks for helping out if the practice hasn't been done yet:

THINK HEIGHT, NOT VELOCITY

There is a common misconception about how to effectively play quietly on a kit drum. Our natural human reaction when thinking about playing at a lower volume is to focus on the velocity that we are striking the drums. Our initial instinct is to try and play quieter by hitting the drums softer. It makes perfect sense. The only issue with this is that we are completely changing how we play because we are focussing on constantly slowing the stick down before we hit the drum to ensure it isn't too loud! Playing in this way affects our timing, our creative ideas, and our control over the instrument because it isn't a natural way of playing.

There is a much more effective way of playing quietly: Don't think about the velocity that you strike the drum at, think about the height that you are allowing your stick to come up to. It is impossible to play loudly if you refuse to bring the stick any higher than an inch from the drum head. It is also impossible to play quietly if you are bringing the stick up a few inches higher than your shoulder!

Consciously keeping the stick low to the drum takes less mental effort and awareness than trying to play every stroke softly. Therefore, we have enough mental space left to focus on what we are playing and not how we are playing it. This can be easily practiced on a practice pad or drum kit, just don't allow the sticks to come further than an inch from the drum or cymbal. Keep that drumstick low!

THE SIZE OF YOUR DRUM STICKS

As drummers, our drumsticks are the tools of our trade, as they are the connection to our instrument. Because of this, it is a really bad habit to change the sticks we use to always fit our situation. In an ideal world, we would have complete control over our technique and playing so that one stick can still accommodate us regardless of the dynamic setting.

However, this can take years of practice which may not be available, so a quick alternative is to change the tools that we are using. Gravity can sometimes play a big part in our technique, so using it to our advantage can get good results.

If you are in a situation where you need to play quietly but haven't yet practiced it enough, then use the next best alternative; basic physics.

The bigger the stick (a 2B stick), the more weight is being moved around and dropped on the drum head. The smaller the stick (a 7A), the less weight is being moved around and being dropped. But this is a last minute substitute! Practicing is still the number one option for best results.

IF TECHNIQUE ISNT QUITE THERE YET, USE HOTRODS

We have discussed using smaller sticks to help us play quieter, but there is another alternative when drum sticks are still too loud. But this is an absolute last resort because it can be one step forward and two steps back.

The alternative to drumsticks are called Hot-Rods. Hot-Rods are still classed as drumsticks, but instead of being a single piece of wood, they are made using multiple dowels of wood. Firstly, by having a stick made of multiple thin pieces of wood, you lose a lot of weight when compared to a normal stick.

Secondly, Hot-Rods do not have the small tips that drumsticks have. This means that the surface area that is striking the drum has more spread, so isn't as loud. This all sounds great and works as an excellent substitute if you just aren't getting the low volume you need when using sticks. The negative to using Hot-Rods instead of sticks is that they completely change the tone and sound of the drums.

They still work great on cymbals, but the tone of the drums will become very thin, with a subtle 'slap' sound when you play them. It is a case of weighing up the priorities, and deciding what your band would like more; great sound or quiet volume.

DAMPENING THE SNARE DRUM AND CYMBALS

Snare drums and cymbals are the two main components of a kit that really cut through the mix. Regarding frequency, they are on the higher end of the spectrum, which means that they are what naturally stands out. In a large church setting where microphones and amplifiers are present, this isn't much of an issue as you can boost the lower frequencies through the mixing desk. But when playing in a smaller setting, the nare and cymbals can start to create a problem when their volumes are uncontrollable.

There is a great trick for getting a Snare Drum to blend nicely into a quieter mix. There are three basic steps; step one is to tune the top head nice and low. Step two is to put lots of dampening onto the snare head (Dampening Gels, Duct Tape, etc).

Step three is to use the tip of your drumstick in the centre of the drum head (no rimshots). By tuning the top head low, you are reducing the attack and cut (how much it cuts through the mix) that the Snare will produce. By heavily dampening a low tuned Snare you will remove all the ringing overtones and create a really 'dead' sounding drum. Also, by not using rimshots you will lose a lot of the harsh attack and bite that a snare drum can give.

Applying these tricks to your Snare Drum means it will sit nicer in the mix, so hopefully the other musicians and congregation won't whine every time you play it. You can even apply this dampening method to your cymbals. Throwing some dampening pads on top can lose some of the over-ring, or in some cases, put some strips of duct tape underneath the cymbal. (Ideally on cymbals that you are not that sentimentally connected to, or that aren't super expensive.)

THE DRUM KIT ALTERNATIVES

As drummers, we usually sigh at the idea that sometimes a full drum kit just isn't needed. We might be playing in a church where a full kit would take up too much room, drown out the rest of the band, or sound out of place when the only other instrument being used is a piano. Although playing a full drum kit is fun there are alternatives, that when approached properly and musically, can really bring something else to the table.

Here are some excellent 'Drum Kit Alternatives':

CAJON

Pronounced 'Ca-Hon', this Wooden Box is an excellent substitute for a drum kit for many reasons. The main one being that even though it only has one playing surface, it can still cover a similar range of frequencies that a drum kit can. When striking the centre of the panel, you will find a nice bass tone, and when striking the top of the panel, you'll find a nice short 'slap' tone. Playing with one or two fingers gets a different sound than slapping with all of your fingers, which gets a different sound from playing with your palm of your hand.

When you combine all of the factors, you end up with a lot of different tonal options and variety of potential frequencies. These Boxes are incredibly portable, easily fit into small spaces, are even easier to put microphones on. They can still provide enough tonal options to make it a great alternative to a drum kit. The price ranges dramatically, but the cheaper options can still sound pretty good, so go grab one!

A SHAKER

This can be one of the most underrated yet useful instruments to use in a small venue or room. Shakers come in many sizes and all sound slightly different. Egg-Shakers are very small but can still add something when the room we are playing in is a small one. Using a shaker is a way of keeping something rhythmic happening throughout a song, without being too intrusive or obvious.

Our role as drummers is to be the timekeeper for the rest of the band, so a shaker can be the next best thing when a drum kit is just too loud. They can be surprisingly difficult to master though, so there is sometimes a need to practice using a shaker to understand the feel of it, and how to effectively keep time with it. The general use is to shake it at the rate of 16th notes and accent where the snare backbeat would usually be, and that is what takes practice to do well! Worship leaders love them though, so crack on.

TAMBOURINE

Depending on whose hands it is in, a tambourine can very easily be a musician's worst nightmare. They can be loud, irritating, in your face, and over used (Can you tell I'm slightly bitter towards tambourines. Bad experiences are tough to forget…). BUT, when used tastefully and musically, these plastic rings with metal disks can add another layer to a small band. At its most basic function, you can use it to replace where the Snare Drum would be.

Using it to give a solid backbeat also gives a sense of time keeping. Alternatively, you can use it in a similar way to a shaker by shaking it at the rate of 16th notes, and on beats 2 and 4 hitting it against your hand to simulate a backbeat. When used well, these things can be gold.

SNARE DRUM AND BRUSHES

This is a drum kit alternative that you don't see that often in churches, but is something that is not used enough. A snare drum, when played with Brushes (sticks with thin, retractable metal wires), can give a similar sound as a Shaker, but with more variety for backbeats, rhythms, and tones. To really get into playing with Brushes, check out some of the top Jazz Drummers who are exceptionally musical with their brush playing.

It can also give some interesting ideas for how to apply using brushes in a small venue. You can drag the brushes around the snare head, strike the drum like you would with a stick, quietly play 16th notes to create a shaker sound, roll the brush over the head, or play different accents and rhythms. The possibilities really are endless, which is why it can be a great substitute for a full drum kit.

THE IMPACT OF PERCUSSION

To put it plainly, percussion can be equally as influential as playing a full drum kit. But only when it is given the appropriate respect and musicality that it deserves. One musical situation that really drives home the importance of every single note we play as drummers is Musical Theatre. If you find the opportunity to play in a musical, then definitely jump at it, because it really highlights how important the little things are when we are playing percussion or drums. Waiting for 64 bars to play a single triangle hit isn't uncommon, but if you miss that hit then it can be so noticeable!

Applying this thinking to when we play percussion in churches can be the difference between serving minimally or serving at our best. A strong attitude and mindset to bear in mind when playing percussive instruments is to THINK MUSICALLY. Knowing when to add, and when to take away musical layers is the key to playing percussion well.

Always be considerate about whether you are adding something to the music or just getting in the way. It is ok to not be playing sometimes if the music requires minimalistic instrumentation. It is easier to start playing with more dynamics if you are already playing minimally. A lot of drummers tend to 'max out' too early and have no more room to dynamically build (this applies to using a full kit as well).

However, if the song needs to lift and needs another layer, then be wise about what you choose to use in order to do this. Being musical in our drumming is key to playing well. Being sensitive, considerate, and musically aware is what can separate the poor percussionists from the percussionists that get called back. Percussion is a great world to explore and can really shift how you think as a musician, which in turn will effect your overall drumming. Great stuff!

MINIMAL MICROPHONES

You are playing in a church that is held in a small room or intimate space, but the sound guy has a spare microphone that you can use. But only one! Is it worth bothering, and if so where is the best place to put it and why would we need to use a microphone?

Even though the space is very small, a microphone can still be really useful. More so because you can use it to either add depth or pick out the subtler instruments so that they cut through the mix. In these situations, microphones are used more to add texture than to project or amplify. Here are some ideas:

MIKING THE CAJON

If we have a microphone available to use with our Cajon, the best place to use it is in the sound hole at the back of the Box. This is because when we look at the variety of frequencies available and how much they project, the higher frequencies will travel through a room easily compared to the lower frequencies. So, when miking a Cajon with only one microphone, it is wise to use it to help the lower frequencies reach the rest of the room. This immediately adds more depth to your Cajon sound, which when played musically can add a lot more dynamic and texture to your overall sound.

MIKING MULTIPLE INSTRUMENTS

If you have one mic available and you are playing tambourines or shakers, it is best to use it as an overhead mic. Overhead microphones sit above a multitude of instruments so that you can switch between what you are using and just play them directly under a microphone. It works better when using lots of different instruments due to the fact you are not individually miking each instrument.

This works great when holding a shaker in one hand and a tambourine in the other. It is important to approach this differently to a usual microphone situation. In most other scenarios the microphone is positioned to accommodate the instrument. In this setting, you need to move your instruemtns to accomdoate the micrphone.

We put microphones onto drums, into the back of a cajon, in front of a singer, etc. In this situation, it is best to have an overhead microphone set up and then we MOVE our instruments INTO its pick-up space. This means that we have to become aware of where our playing is happening in relation to the microphone. It results in the ability to switch between various instruments and accommodate the sound engineer by mixing ourselves, depending on how close or far we play from the microphone.

HYMNS VS CONTEMPORARY WORSHIP

This is quite a tricky subject to write about, simply because the term 'Hymn' is excruciatingly broad and quite vague. So in order to give some insight into this topic, there will sadly have to be a large amount of generalisation to avoid listing every hymn ever written and picking them apart one by one.

To give some context, I am going to be focussing on the musical style of songs written by the likes of John and Charles Wesley, Isaac Watts, or John Newton. It's great to be aware of songs such as *And Can It Be,*

Amazing Grace, Be Still For The Presence Of The Lord, Be Thou My Vision, Thine Be The Glory, and *How Great Thou Art.* We will also be looking into the style of more modern songs that have a certain 'Hymn-Feel' to them and talk about why that is. Songs such as *In Christ Alone, How Deep The Fathers Love For Us* or *Be Still For The Presence Of The Lord.* (By the term 'modern' I mean post 1980's…)

Hymns can potentially be a genuine fear for drummers, and in some cases rightly so. Traditional Hymns, sometimes sung a few hundred years ago, were written in a time where instrumentation and musicianship were approached very differently. One reason that drummers feel anxious when asked to play Hymns is simply because we have very little context; we are being asked to play songs that were not necessarily written with drums in mind.

With the ever-evolving movement of contemporary and modern worship music (which has essentially become a genre of its own), it can be easy to overlook traditional hymns and class them as out of date or 'too old'. The first big observation when looking at Hymns is that some of our greatest worship music today was inspired and influenced by those traditional pieces. When you really look into the lyrics and the musicianship within some of those classic hymns, they can be truly incredible! (I specifically say SOME, I'm aware of the more 'Dirge' style hymns that are less popular for various reasons…)

One potential reason why hymns aren't used as much today, could be simply becuase they don't give the same impact stylistically that they did at the time they were written. But this is where the challenge comes; just because they were written with a different sound, does that mean we should exclude them from our worship times? I would say definitely not. Lyrically, some Hymns carry real power and are incredibly moving pieces.

As the united church, we preach the same gospel and the same message of Jesus, yet we are forever finding new ways to deliver that message. Hymns should be approached in exactly the same way. The message, lyrics, and melodies within some of those old songs are beautiful, but how we play and deliver them is what we can change. So, as drummers, how do we approach playing this 'stylistically different' form of music? Here are some tips, advice, and ideas;

FIND THE PULSE

This is always the starting point, and for playing Hymns it is crucial. It is not uncommon for Hymns to have been written using multiple time signatures, interesting chord changes, and complex timings. So, before we try and play anything remotely interesting, we need to be able to keep time while the Hymn is being sung. In some cases, this is all that's needed throughout the whole piece, just a reference of time for the rest of the band and congregation to lock on to.

If we can find the pulse within a Hymn, we then have the option to play something more interesting if it is needed. However, if we can't find a solid pulse then we shouldn't even consider playing anything, as it will inevitably sound messy. Common timings found in Hymns are 6/8, 3/4 and 2/4, and it is not uncommon for the time signature to be different for one bar! So, finding what time signature the Hymn is in is a great start, and whether you can keep some form of pulse throughout.

LISTEN TO THE CHORD CHANGES

This could be considered a sweeping statement but I'm going to say it anyway; In most contemporary worship music, the musicality and chords used can usually be quite predictable.

This means that they are usually easy to follow and to play over. One big difference between Contemporary Worship and Hymns is that the chords and rhythms used can have a very different feel to them. The musicality of Hymns and how the chords were constructed can sometimes be rhythmically confusing and musically compelling!

When playing Hymns, it is essential to really listen to what the rest of the instruments are doing. Notice where the chords change are and what rhythm is being used to move them. As drummers, we play an instrument that isn't pitched, so worrying about chords and notes can sometimes slip our minds, but by being aware of the chord changes we can ensure that we follow the same rhythm and overall feel of the hymn. It can be the main difference between a hymn sounding great, or sounding messy and dis-organised.

STRAIGHT GROOVES SOMETIMES DONT WORK

This is a really interesting idea and can be one of the hardest aspects of playing Hymns, especially when we are so used to Contemporary Worship. Sometimes a straight, repetitive groove just doesn't work. The way that Hymns are written involves having phrases, melodic expressions, and musical riffs throughout that can change and flow. In one sense it is beautiful and a sign of incredible musicianship from the composer, but for drummers it can be a nightmare.

We have drilled into our mindset from day one that counting is everything for playing drums, and keeping a straight and consistent groove or rhythm is essential. And yet in some Hymns, this just doesn't work.

An example of this is one of my all-time favourite songs; *In Christ Alone*. Lyrically it is incredible, the melody is exceptional, and the overall dynamic flow is outstanding! But it is a song that so many drummers shy away from because of its 'Hymn-like' rhythm and timing. This is an example where playing a straight groove the whole way through can appear to sound ok, and then suddenly not sound right. This is because of certain phrases and timings found within the song. Here is the way of approaching it (it is probably the most 'hippie-like' thing I will ever say), but you really need to FEEL the music, not COMPLICATE it. What I mean by this is not to try and figure out how it all pieces together and how you are going to count your way through it.

The reason "*In Christ Alone*" has such a strong 'Hymn vibe' is because the melody and lyrics are what carries it. So, this how we need to approach it as drummers. I never count while playing this song, I sing along and let my limbs follow the lyrical and melodic rhythms. My right hand becomes my pulse that my other limbs follow and play around, pulling out backbeats where it seems appropriate and putting a bass drum where I feel the start of a bar or phrase is. It is tricky and takes practice, but in a simple nutshell it is just a different mindset to playing Contemporary Worship.

UNDERSTAND THE LYRICS AND EMOTION THAT THE COMPOSER WAS CAPTURING

This should be applied to all music that we play, but more so with traditional hymns. What emotion is the composer trying to capture with this Hymn? Lyrically this becomes incredibly obvious which is really helpful. Composers who spent their life writing Hymns had a real gift for how they worked lyrics together and managed to say a lot within one verse. So really understanding what you are playing and how you can add appropriate drum ideas to that Hymn is a great attitude.

As we read before, a lot of Hymns were written without any drums to accompany it, which means we sometimes have to add our own ideas. Knowing the lyrics and what the composer was trying to capture is the first step to adding something rhythmic. Our playing needs to enhance the Hymn, not detract from the desired emotion or message.

*

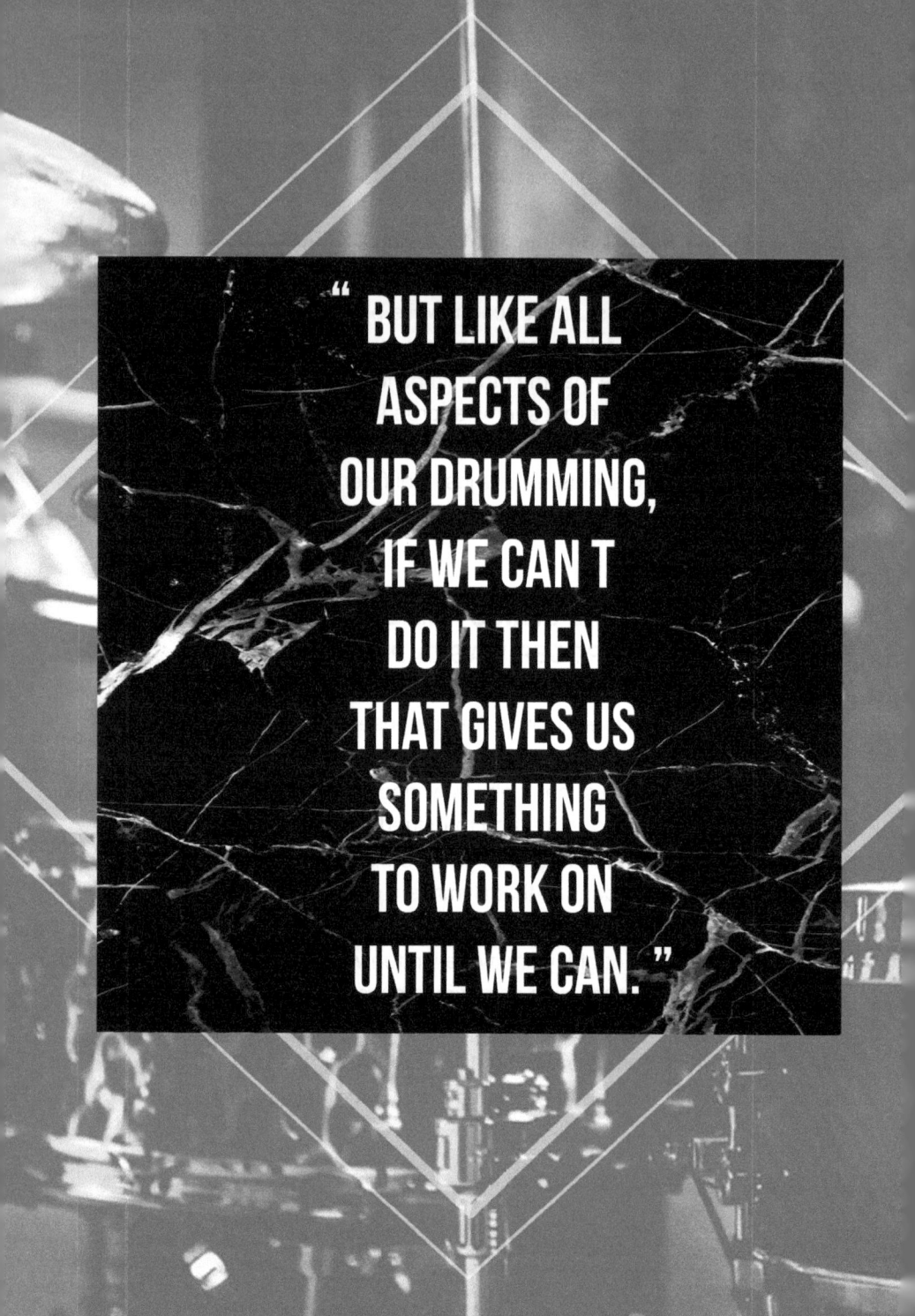

> "BUT LIKE ALL ASPECTS OF OUR DRUMMING, IF WE CAN'T DO IT THEN THAT GIVES US SOMETHING TO WORK ON UNTIL WE CAN."

EIGHT
THE HYBRID DRUMMER

8

THE HYBRID DRUMMER
WHERE ACOUSTIC AND ELECTRONIC MEET

This chapter was fairly late to the party when writing this book but thankfully it made the cut as it is a really useful tool for creating various musical atmospheres. It is the concept of mixing acoustic real-life drums, with electronically sampled sounds. Using one without the other can still go a long way, but when we start looking at using both elements together it opens up a whole new world of creative freedom.

Incorporating electronics into our playing can be a daunting idea. If that is the case for you then do not feel ashamed of that apprehensive feeling. As drummers, we are used to playing an instrument that requires no electricity at all; a completely acoustic instrument. So when we think about adding new drums, cymbals, or percussion to our set up it is usually really exciting. However, the idea of adding something that is essentially disconnected to the core value of our instrument can lead to some nervousness.

But have no fear! Looking into how to start bringing some electronics into your worship can be really fun if you dive straight in. I have met numerous drummers who were intimidated by the concept of drum electronics, who now thoroughly enjoy using them (there are also a few who still hate them, but we won't talk about them…). In this chapter we are going to explore various foundational electronic ideas, how to effectively use them, and how to avoid or fix potential problems or experiences.

ELECTRONIC DRUM KITS

Electronic Drum Kits sometimes get a bad press when they are used in a live setting. Even though there are some companies that have really made some strong headway with the sounds available, they still have a very different tone and feel to an acoustic kit. Having said all of that, there can sometimes be a real place and need for electronic drums. Especially when we consider combining them with our main drum kits. As with most things in life, there can be pros and cons when using electric kits in worship. Whether it be stand-alone or combined with an acoustic drum kit, let's see what is available:

STAND ALONE ELECTRIC KIT

It isn't uncommon for a drummer to find themselves in the position where an electronic kit is the only option. It can come down to anything from financial restrictions, volume problems, lack of space or how portable the kit needs to be. If an electric drum kit is the easiest option for a church, there are still ways of getting the best from it and making a pleasing sound when you play.

One of the main problems, when a drummer plays an electric kit in a small space, is that they can forget that there will still be a sound when the stick hits the rubber pad. It can defeat the point of using an electric kit to minimise volume issues if the thudding of wood on rubber is still very apparent. Be mindful of the tapping of your drumstick on the rubber pad. If you are playing in a larger space then it won't be a problem, but if your church venue is small and intimate then it can be a better idea to play softer on the rubber pads and turn the general volume up through the PA.

When it comes to the sounds that you use on your electric kit the aim of the game is to provide the right tone for the room you are in. Now some electric kits don't allow you much freedom to change the sound of the drums or sometimes you will just be given 10 preset kit sounds. In these situations, you just have to pick the one that sounds best in your opinion. In a circumstance where your electric kit allows you some creative control, it is possible to get your electric kit sounding great for your church.

This paragraph could easily be a list of thousands of potential sound options, but to avoid tons of possibilities it is better to give a concept. Think about the room that your church is in and what acoustic drum kit would work in that room. It can be really un-nerving when a team who meet in a small room are using an electric kit with loud, heavy, stadium rock drum sounds. The two environments don't work together so it feels uncomfortable… If a church has a large space and big PA, but the electronic drums sound like a small Bop Jazz Kit then the same reaction can happen.

Choose the kit sounds that work with the room you are meeting in.

COMBINED WITH YOUR MAIN KIT

Using electronics with acoustic instruments is one of the main avenues that contemporary worship music is exploring, when wanting to push the boundaries of sound cappabilities. It is a great way to take the elements of worship music that we are already familiar with and merge them with exciting layers. It is becoming more and more common to see electronic components on drum kits in both a church and non-church environment.

Drum electronics can be a vast and overcrowded market, ranging from sample pads, triggers, electronic drum heads, and Octo-Pads etc… If it is something that you are exploring, then there are good starting points for incorporating some electronics into your acoustic kit set up. The main thing to bear in mind is that the electronics are there to work alongside your main kit, so they both need to exist in harmony together.

It is when drummers are unable to create an equal partnership between these elements that confusion, frustration, and eventually rejection of electronics happens. It can be a real waste of potential possibilities… So an easy first step is to take components of an electric drum kit and blend them into your acoustic kit. It is a really simple process and begins by choosing one or two pads from your electric kit.

The handy thing about most electric kits is that you can move the pads anywhere you want or even put them on a separate stand. As long as they are still connected to the kits module (brain), you are able to plug it into the PA and therefore still make noise. So the trick is to take one or two pads, connect them to a different stand, and position them somewhere on your kit that you can reach easily, that also doesn't get in the way of the main drums. As long as the module is somewhere in the vicinity (having it on the floor will still work) then you have something to plug the pads into and assign a sound to. Plug the module into your PA with a Direct Input Box (DI Box) and then you are good to go!

This can open up a whole world of possibilities for adding different sounds to your kit. This is true when we consider the number of percussive instruments that could be used and how impractical it would be to have all of those instruments in our playing space. Cowbells, Tambourines, Triangles, Small Snare Drums, Wood Blocks, Click, Timpani, and Gongs are now all possible with the two extra pads you have added to your drum kit. (I would dare anyone to try and bring an actual 12 foot Gong into their church!)

The main problem that you and the sound engineer will need to monitor are the levels, and that the acoustic and electronic drums are mixed together evenly.

Explore the sounds on the module, be creative and have fun with it!

SAMPLE PADS & CHOOSING SOUNDS

Sample Pads are becoming an integral live component of certain genres and musical situations because of the diverse possibilities that they offer. A Sample Pad is essentially a box with multiple pads on them that you can assign a different sound to. This means that instead of having to set up 9 different pads around your kit, you now have all 9 pads on one box. Coming from the previous paragraph, there are a lot of similarities between adding pads from an electric kit and adding a Sample Pad into your set up.

The general process is the same; find a space on your kit to add your Sample Pad, plug the pad into a DI box which then plugs into the PA system, then you're good to go! Once you have added it to your drum kit, the fun begins because there is a large difference between a Sample Pad and the preset electric kit pads. You can assign your OWN sounds to a Sample Pad.

This means you now have the possibility of creating or downloading a desired sound and uploading it onto one of the available pads. This opens up a whole new world of creative and experimental capabilities! The tricky bit is creating the sounds, but there is plenty of music software available to assist this. It is a wonderful feeling when you have a certain snare sound that you know would work perfectly with a certain song and you either download or create it, then simply upload it to your Sample Pad to use until you delete it. Once you get comfortable and experienced using a Sample Pad, worship leaders will really enjoy its capabilities and will love the creative freedom you can now offer the team.

One way of viewing the function of a Sample Pad is that it can be used to create a completely different environment or atmosphere. The joy is that a 'sample' can be as long or short as you like. So something like a Gong sample can finish quickly or have a long sustain depending on what you think would work. By having control over the sounds you can upload and use means that you can provide exactly the vibe that your worship team is after. Here are some ideas and categories to get you started:

ATMOSPHERICAL: Gongs, Reverse Cymbals, reverberating bass drums, echoey clicks, drones, cymbals with effects.

BIG & ECHOEY SOUNDS: A Snare with tons of reverb, an echoey snap, a large floor tom that sounds like it is being played in a large cave!

TIGHT SOUNDS: A really dry and tight Snare drum, various hand claps, electronic 'club style' Snare Drums, 808 Kick Drum, electronic Hi-Hats.

SUB DROPS: A sustained bass note that is lower than a bass guitar can reach. These work amazingly when you land into a dynamically powerful section of a song. There are loads of Sub-Drops available online and although they are great fun, be careful to not overuse them! (I definitely have...)

BACKING TRACKS

Backing Tracks (BT's) can be such a valuable tool for any band in any capacity. It can add so many layers to a song and provide the instrumentation that isn't available to your music team. BT's are essentially tracks that are played from a laptop or sample pad, that the band plays along with. This is so that extra instruments can be added into a song such as strings, synths, sub-bass, and textures. Most BT's have a click/metronome running throughout so that the band can stay in time with the track. It can be tricky at first, but it can also be a brilliant tool if your worship team isn't that big or you would like some additional texture to the songs.

Playing with a BT can be intimidating and slightly alien when you first try it. A common theme throughout this chapter is that there are pro's and cons' of using BT's in worship which we will look at in more detail. The following points will hopefully give some advice and tips for effective use of BT's:

SETTING UP A BACKING TRACK

One of the huge contributing factors to the success and delivery of a backing track is how it is set up. Now this point could go into lots of detail on mixing, mastering, EQ-ing and general technical advice. However, if you really want to get into the ins and outs of this then I would really recommend some extensive study. Check out artists or websites that specialise in that element of music. In this section, we are going to look into two key aspects of setting up backing tracks that can make using them in worship so much easier.

It comes down to two things, how to add a click easily and how to add vocal cues to help the band out. Both are achieved in similar ways. The general idea is that the backing track that you want the congregation to hear, and the track that you want the band to be able to hear need to come from different places. Now without a large mixing desk and musical software being permanently open, this can be tricky. But there is an easier way around it, which is is all about "panning". Panning is basically which speaker (left or right) the music is coming out of. When we listen to music on headphones we are listening to a 'stereo mix' which means the producer would have mixed the track so that certain instruments come through different sides. As we have two ears it makes sense to listen to music through two speakers, which is essentially what headphones are.

This is the important bit about setting up a BT; make sure there is a channel which has the click/metronome on it and then make sure that it is panned either completely left or completely right. If you are listening on headphones then you will only hear the click in one of the earpieces. So if it is played through big speakers it will have the same effect. The next step is when you play it live you need to run it as a stereo track, talk to your sound person and get them to send the left stereo (let's say that has the click on it) to the band members in-ear mix, and send the right stereo (no click) to the front of house speakers. There are multiple ways of doing this which include panning, having an input splitter, using two DI boxes, etc.

For more advice on this topic there are a number of really helpful videos and articles online to search through (loopcommunity.com is a resource that is mentioned a lot). But in a brief nutshell; by utlising panning, the track that is going into the bands in-ears will have a click on it and the track coming out the main speakers won't!

Once we can get this working there is a brilliant addition to just using a click. There is now the option to add voice cues to the track as this will be on the pan side that only the band can hear. This can be good for removing any element of confusion or guesswork regarding where you are in the track. On the last bar of each section of the song basically needs the name or dynamic change of the upcoming section and then a vocal count in. This is achieved by recording your voice giving the vocal cues and then adding them onto the track so that it's in time. For example; "Chorus…2…3…4…" or "drop-out…2…3…4…". By adding these cues your worship leader can clearly communicate where the song is going and what needs to happen. This eliminates any confusion as to where in the song you are or what you need to be playing. Dreamy!

TRIGGERING SECTIONS INSTEAD OF A WHOLE BACKING TRACK
One of the main issues with using BT's in church is that worship works best when it is free and spirit lead. As a BT is not a person, it cannot be changed or communicated with easily and therefore can almost become an anchor. BT's can add so much to the overall sound of a song and can

bring sounds in that cannot be played on instruments, but some worship leaders simply don't enjoy the inflexible nature of them. But there are ways around this, which is known as 'Triggering'. This requires a sample pad and a bit of preparation time!

The general idea is that instead of playing a BT as a whole track from start to finish, you slice the BT into sections and trigger them individually. This means playing to a click can be slightly harder so if you can get a sample pad with a click that comes out on a separate channel then that is really useful (The Roland SPD-SX does this). This means that if your worship leader wants to repeat a section again then you have the ability to follow them by re-triggering that section of the BT. This means there will still be an element of 'spirit lead' worship which is flexible and flows.

To give a quick overview on how to do this; open the BT into some music software, make sure the BPM is right so that all the timing is right and cut up the BT into sections. Intro, Verse, Chorus, Link, Bridge etc. On your sample pad you will need to assign each section onto a different pad (preferably in order to remember which pad has which section on it). Then instead of playing a whole BT you just trigger the appropriate section as and when you need to. This will take practice but can become second nature.

A POTENTIAL PROBLEM & SOLUTIONS

This is something that is really important to talk about; what do we do when something goes wrong and we are playing with a backing track. This point zeroes in on a really common problem when playing with a BT; the worship leader or singer has started singing at the wrong point so is now out of place with the BT…

The essence of playing with backing tracks is that you are essentially bound to a set structure that is unchangeable. So what happens when something goes wrong and we are playing against an unchangeable component?? As drummers, we are usually the first port of call to fix a problem or complication so it is good to try and get the band back on the track as quickly as you can. How we play can be a massive tool for giving signals to other band members; a key element of our playing that is helpful here is our drum fills. If we have found ourselves in a situation where we are playing to a backing track but our worship leader has started singing to early so is ahead of the BT, our fills can signal that something is out. If a singer is singing a line and then suddenly hears a drum fill in the middle of their lyric they will usually turn to the drummer slightly disgruntled. In a situation where a singer is out of place with the backing track then that is exactly what you want! They should be aware that you are in full control of the track, so if something doesn't sound right then it is most likely the band, not the track. Once they realise something is out, the trick is to keep playing small drum fills to signify where the start of the bar or section is. Show them where beat 1 is by filling into it until they pick it back up.

Alternatively, if you know the lyrics to the song well then simply mouthing the words along to the backing track can be enough to get a worship leader back on the right path. The main thing to remember when playing to a backing track is to stick to what you know is right and stay glued to the track. If the drummer falls away from the backing track then the band is in for a world of problems, whereas if the drummer can stay with it then other musicians can correct themselves quicker to get back to where the track is. You need to become their reference point.

Absolute worse case scenario; Stop the track. But this is an absolute last resort and shouldn't be done in a moment of panic! If something has gone so wrong and it is proving impossible to fix then just stop the track and finish the song without it. If the track is such an integral part to the song then end the song smoothly where you are and then restart the track. It will sound like a deliberate decision or that you are just repeating a section of a song. Having said this, 9 out of 10 times there is a solution that can be found if the drummers remains calm and thinks clearly.

CLICK PRACTICE

It is at this point in the chapter that my 'inner-drum-teacher' has got the better of me and I couldn't help but give some practice material. To get comfortable playing to a backing track you need to be comfortable playing to a click. There is a difference between being able to stay in time with the click, and being able to not think about staying in time with the click.

"Comfortable" by definition means to provide physical ease and relaxation, so if we are apprehensive using a click or having to use tons of concentration then that is a sign we are not comfortable. But like all aspects of our drumming, if we can't do it then that gives us something to work on until we can. Practice is the key to progressing in any skill or craft, and becoming a drummer that can play to a click while not really noticing it is definitely a desirable and achievable goal. Here are a few simple exercises that can develop your time and awareness of the click:

1. SUBDIVISION WITH CLICK (beginner)

This exercise is the simplest one but also so key for developing the ability to play well with a click. One key problem drummers face when playing with a click is that they become aware of just how much their timing quickens or slows down. The main culprit for this effect is subdivisions and how competent we are at switching between them.

That is what this exercise works on and it's dead simple; it is about choosing a tempo and then working up a subdivision pyramid. Start the click at a chosen tempo (i.e 80 bpm) then play 4 bars of 1/4 notes, 4 bars of 8th notes, 4 bars of Triplets, 4 bars of 16th notes and 4 bars of 16th Note Triplets. Once you reach the end, work your way back down to 1/4 notes again. So the order of subdivisions goes as follows:
1/4 > 8th's > Triplets > 16th's > Sextuplets > 16th's > Triplets > 8th's > 1/4

How you choose to play these subdivisions is your creative freedom and has vast possibilities. Play them as single strokes on your snare or practice pad, play them as a groove, or even play them as different drum fills!

The trick is once you are comfortable playing 4 bars each time you then reduce to 3 bars, and then 2, and then 1, then reduce each subdivision to 2 beats, then to only one beat! Being able to flow easily through subdivisions is an amazing skill that will not only work on your click playing but also your overall timing, control, and general drumming ability.

2. GAP CLICK (intermediate)

This exercise is brilliant for developing a great sense of "inner-time". It is a simple yet effective exercise which involves setting a metronome up so that it audibly plays a set number of bars and then mutes another number of bars. A 'gap click' is exactly that, it puts a gap in the sound so that you have to continue without being able to hear the click.

Start by trying to play a groove along with 3 bars of click and then one bar of silence. It is all about keeping your tempo solid and consistent even when you can't hear the click. Then increase it to 2 bars on, 2 bars off. Then for the tricky exercise which is 1 bar on, 3 bars off! Once you feel your grooves are solid and consistent then its time to start trying some drum fills as well. It is a really tricky, but really useful, exercise that you can apply to any practice material that you are working on! Being able to quickly adjust our timing to correct the inconsistencies of our tempo is essential for effectively playing with a click. The joy with this exercise is the dramatic change you will see in your drumming when a click isn't even involved. The more you work on this stuff, the more your inner tempo will be sharpened. You can find a number of apps or websites that can provide a 'gap click'. A quick google search should bring up the latest and most up to date link.

3. CLICK DISPLACEMENT (ADVANCED)

This exercise isn't something you would use in a live setting, but it is excellent for becoming completely aware of the click and your tempo. Naturally we hear the click as the downbeat in a bar, meaning that we hear the click on 1, 2, 3, 4 which tells us where the main pulse is. This exercise explores moving the click so that it falls on a different measure in a beat. On one hand it is a completely pointless exercise because if you ever play live with a click then it will be there to signal where the downbeat is. So surely it is pointless to practice with the click on a different point in the beat?

The reason this is a brilliant exercise is because it is impossible to do unless you're timing is spot on and your subdivisions are super clean. By shooting at a moving target, you are actually improving your ability to land a bullseye on a stationary one because your body is learning to adapt and modify itself while in motion! Tricky stuff, but so good.

The easiest of the click transitions is to move the click onto the offbeat. A simple technique for doing this is to play your standard 8th note drum beat and count beat 1 twice! This means you will play two bass drums, and the second will become the start of the bar and the click will be sounding on the '+'s of the bar. The advanced exercises are moving the click onto the other 16th notes (the 'e' and the 'a' of a beat). To move it onto the 'e', just play a drum beat but count 16th notes over it. When you get to beat 4 don't play the last 16th (the 'a'). If you count '4 e + **1**' and then drop the bass drum back where 'a' should be then the click will be on the 'e' of the beat. To put the click on the last 16th you can use the same system, but you need to start with the click on the offbeat, miss off the last 16th, and voila!

It's all very techy and nerdy, so don't stress about it! It's fun and a great exercise but its also very tricky so don't break an arm over it! If you're bored or you need some more click practice then give it a go! Check out some YouTube videos on 'moving the click' and prepare for amazment.

DRUM TRIGGERS

Slightly different to the style of 'Triggering', but also slightly similar. A Drum Trigger is a device that clips onto a drum and then runs a signal through a console or sound source. This means that when you play the drum normally, a sound effect will also be triggered at the same time. This is essentially removing the need to strike a separate pad if you want an effect added to one of your drums. This works great for adding reverb to a Snare Drum, extra bass to a kick drum, or even more 'thump' to your Big Tom!

This is what is considered 'Layering' as you are adding additional texture to your already existing drum sound, without the need for any extra pads. This is essentially the definition of being a 'Hybrid Drummer'. You are combining electronic devices with the acoustic elements of your kit to deliver a certain sound.

This can be a big world to explore though, so as a starting point we are going to look at adding a side snare to your kit. It is super simple, all you need is a second snare drum, a drum trigger, and a sound source. The idea is that you set up your second snare drum on your kit and tune it slightly differently to your main snare drum. You then add a drum trigger to it and assign a sound from the sound source. Let's use an example and say we will apply a reverb/echoey snare sound to the trigger. This now gives us the option to use our primary snare drum and also our second snare, which has an echo on it to give us two sound possibilities! This provides endless ideas for sounds and subtle textures and layers.

You can even create a silent version of this by using a second Snare Drum shell, a special drum head, your trigger, and a sound source. The special head you need to get is called a "mesh head', which is a drum head that makes practically no noise when you strike it. Because of this, it means you can add a trigger to this new snare and choose a desired sound. So when you strike this snare, you will hear the sound that comes from the module, but not an actual snare sound!

This is great if you need a clap sound, a disco snare, an extra tom, a sub drop, etc. The possibilities are endless! For more info, check out companies like Roland, Yamaha or Alesis and see their wealth of information on drum triggers.

DRUMS SCREENS

This paragraph is being put into this chapter simply because it has been tricky to find anywhere else to put it. Yet it is pretty important information and a question that many Church goers ask; why is the drummer inside a large clear box?

The big misconception to immediately rectify is this; they are not soundproof. The clear drum screens are there to reduce the higher frequencies. High frequencies travel further but also don't travel through solid material as easily. It is the reason that if you stand outside a club or venue, you can hear the bass but not treble. So the clear screen is there to stop vocalist microphones picking up the cymbals. It makes the drum kit easier to mic as it isolates the sound around the drums. Sound guys usually love them as it also makes the overall stage sound easier to mix.

They can be very sweaty in the summer and can make you feel slightly disconnected from the other musicians, but it's also like having your very own cave/den to hang out in so it can be fun!

*

"A FIELD MANUAL;
BECAUSE IT NEEDS TO BE TAKEN INTO THE FIELD"

"...WE ARE USUALLY THE FIRST CALL WHEN A WORSHIP LEADER WANTS TO CREATE A DIFFERENT DYNAMIC OR MUSICAL DECISION."

NINE
TERMINOLOGY

THE FIELD
MANUAL

9

THE TERMINOLOGY

WHAT WORSHIP LEADERS ARE ASKING FOR AND HOW TO MAKE IT HAPPEN

There is a reason (sadly) that there are so many drummer jokes flying around the internet and musically sociable places. Naturally, our instrument involves hitting something with a stick. It can appear to be a very 'caveman-ish' practice that requires no skill or musical knowledge. As long as you can repeatedly count to 4, and don't try to play anything too 'musical' then you can be a drummer! Having said that some of the jokes are getting pretty clever...

But when all jokes are put aside, most musicians who know anything about music will be aware of how important drums are within a musical setting and how unique this instrument is. When playing in a band, so much of the power, sound, and feel comes from the drummer. This is why we are usually the first call when a worship leader wants to create a different dynamic or musical decision. If the drummer understands and can make it happen, then the rest of the musicians having something to jump onto, making the whole band sound unified as a result.

The problem arises when a musician that is not a drummer wants to request that the drummer does something and just can't quite figure out how to verbalise it. Or more commonly, the worship leader will ask for a certain emotion or feeling to be musically captured which then becomes our job as drummers to make happen. This can be tricky though!

If there was ever a reason to keep this book permanently in your stick bag, it is this chapter! The number of drummers who have been heard saying something along the lines of "Why can't you put what you're asking for into drummer terms/language?". Well that is exactly what this chapter is for! Below is a list of commonly used emotional and stylistic requests that have come from worship leaders, followed by how to practically play differently in order to give them what they want. If your worship leader asks for a specific feel for a song, fly through the book to this chapter and discover how you actually make a song sound more *"oomphy"*...

POTENTIAL REQUESTS

ATMOSPHERIC
'relating to the atmosphere of the earth'
Think less about keeping straight and solid time! Think more about being percussive and creating sound effects. Swirling cymbals, rolling Toms, and rhythms on the Snare drum with the Snare wires off all work great. Avoid a straight groove unless it is specifically asked for. This is all about playing into the spaces and avoiding too much structure or pulse.

DECLARATIVE
'of the nature of or making a declaration.'
No one ever 'declares' anything quietly or subtly, otherwise it would just be considered a weak statement. To declare something requires some power and boldness, and that is how your drumming should sound. Keep the groove super simple but give it some power! A strong backbeat, not too many ghost notes, and a very straight Kick pattern should all work. If you add too much then it will sound busy and potentially quite funky. There is a difference between playing with power and playing loudly. Keeping the groove sparse but strong means you won't have to beat the life out of the kit, which just adds volume.

ENERGETIC
'showing or involving great activity or vitality.'
This can either mean the worship leader would like you to play slightly faster, or to add more energy to the groove itself. Double up something within the groove; if you are playing 1/4 notes on the Hi-Hat, then double it to 8th Notes. If you aren't using any Ghost Notes then start adding them in! Give your groove more energy by creating a sense of urgency and slight busyness. This might not mean you need to play faster, just add more elements and layers into your groove. 16th notes on the Hi-Hat usually does the trick!

EXCITING
'causing great enthusiasm and eagerness'
To play excitably doesn't mean overplaying! This is about creating an environment where your congregation joins in with your excitement! A '4-on-the-floor' groove always achieves this! '4-on-thefloor' means you play your Bass drum on the 1/4 notes, and your snare on 2 and 4. Think of the majority of EDM tracks (Electronic Dance Music) or Superstition by Stevie Wonder. The reason this works so well is becuase it is a groove that is simple enough to not confuse anyone, but with enough happening to get people excited and expectant. It's why so many pop songs and wedding set lists involve this groove!

'GIVE SPACE'
'a continuous area or expanse which is free, available, or unoccupied'
UNOCCUPIED is the main word in that definition. In a nutshell, this is a polite way for a worship leader to ask you to stop playing… Just keep time on a Ride Cymbal.

GROOVY
A musical phrase with no dictionary definition. So in context; *"Can you make it more groovy?"*
This is a moment where you don't need to think too much about what you're playing, but rather how you are playing it, and how it feels. For a drum beat to 'groove' it needs to feel great and have people tapping their foot. A great way to make a your beats groove that little bit more is to 'swing it' ever so slightly. This means your groove has a slightly more bouncy sound to it. Play your Hi-Hats louder than usual so that they stand out. Think of funky songs and how great they feel when played well! The 'Half Time Shuffle' is arguably one of the best examples of a drum beat that properly grooves! To get people tapping their foot to your groove it needs to have a sense of trust and predictability, so keep it solid and don't change what you are doing every bar. Pick a groove and stick to it so that everyone else has no unexpected surprises.

MAJESTIC
'Having or showing impressive beauty or scale'
A really useful technique: lower the volume of your cymbals so that the lower frequencies stand out (Kick and Snare) and delay your backbeat slightly. Play a 'flam' between your Snare and a cymbal so that the Snare falls just behind the beat. This can immediately make a groove sound thicker, more majestic and generally grander!

"OOOMPH"...
"the quality of being exciting or energetic."
One sure way to play with 'oomph' is to really mean what you play. A shy musician that is trying not to be heard will inevitably sound weak. Play with confidence, especially if you don't feel confident and play like you mean every single note! Don't creep into any section awkwardly and quietly, use bold and simple fills to flow between sections of a song. Everything you play needs to sound deliberate and intended.

RELAXED
'free from tension and anxiety'
One sure way to create tension is to have too much happening in your playing. Strip it all back and keep it to the basics of the groove, maybe use a cross stick on the Snare or play on top of the Hi-Hat with the tip of your stick instead of using the shoulder. This is about your playing becoming more of a texture than an obvious drum beat. If you want to give a really relaxed feel then delay the backbeat slightly (using a flam between your Snare and Hi-hat) or even swing the groove ever so slightly to give it some bounce. You want the rest of the band to feel calm and safe with the groove you start playing, so keeping the tempo solid and the groove predictable can help with this.

SOLID
'firm and stable in shape; not liquid or fluid'
Keep it simple and don't add anything fancy. Make sure the tempo set in stone and let all the other musicians build on you as their solid foundation. Play with confidence and presence, don't be nervous or try to hide/go unheard. The busier you make your groove then the less comfortable the other musicians or congregation may feel. To give a feeling of solidness in your playing means you need to play a groove that makes the other musicians trust that you aren't going to try anything too outrageous.

STRONG/'WITH STRENGTH'
'having the power to move heavy weights or perform other physically demanding tasks'
In order to give a groove a sense of strength, you need to enhance the main components which are the Bass and Snare. Keep the groove simple and reduce the volume of your Ride and Hi-Hats. This will make your Bass and Snare drum stand out more which will sound stronger, giving the drums more presence and authority. If you are going to use

your crash cymbals then use them sparingly. This means that when you do use them it will add some real weight.

"SIT/LEAN BACK ON IT"

This is more of a phrase than an emotion, but it gets used a lot! If you are ever asked to "Sit on it" or "Lean back on it" or something to that effect, it simply means to stop rushing. It is a visual image of someone relaxing on a chair and not sitting forward/standing with anxiety and tension. So, it is a metaphor for slowing down and keeping the tempo slightly slower than you are currently doing it.

"SWOOSHY"

This isn't actually a word, but is a common 'noise' that worship leaders make when they want a specific sound…
Basically it just means use lots of cymbal swells.

TRIBAL/BATTLE CRY

'of a characteristic of a tribe or tribes
a slogan expressing the ideals of people engaged in a campaign'
Toms Toms Toms Toms and more Toms! Don't think groove, think of rhythms and power on the biggest Tom that you have available. You want people feeling empowered and essentially ready for battle, so imagine the Roman army marching to the sound of a large drum.

Don't overplay and don't think of complex rhythms, think solid and consistent so people can get on board with what you are doing. If it is just you playing this then it is not a solo opportunity, keep the tempo solid and the rhythms simple.
"Celtic' is also a request that falls into this category. Play a groove on the Toms, but it needs to have a lighter and more joyful feel compared to the 'Tribal' sound.

"VIBEY"

'a person's emotional state or the atmosphere of a place as communicated to and felt by others'

I want to give my good friend and amazing worship leader April Ballard credit for this as she uses this phrase all the time and I love it! To 'Vibe' essentially means you are going to sit in a space/atmosphere until further direction comes. This means not overplaying, but also keeping the band together. Keeping time on a cymbal works great, or if you think a groove would work then it needs to be light and minimal. Simplicity is key here; Rim-Clicks sound great if you are going to use a groove. Try and avoid having a backbeat on both 2 and 4, just pick one of them to add some space to the groove. Listen to the other musicians and pick out the rhythms that they are using.

SOME COMMON 'MIS-WORDINGS'

Sometimes when we are given instructions, they are worded in a way that makes sense to the asker but not to a drummer. Sometimes, part of the role of all a musician is to decipher what is being asked, even though it isn't being expressed properly. One of the hardest, yet most crucial, skill of any musician is being able to look past how something is being asked to accommodate the request. This can usually be one of the biggest contributors to band fall out in a practice room, and church music teams are no different. Within this chapter is also included the following section which will hopefully save some time around this subject. If you are being asked something that just isn't making sense, have a quick look through the following section to see if it helps. If not then enjoy the task of deciphering your worship leaders code…

Here are a few thoughts to save some time and energy:

"PLAY FASTER, BUT DON'T SPEED UP"

There is a difference between what sounds faster and what is actually faster. If you are being asked to play faster, and were then told off for speeding up the song too much, then this is a clear sign that you are being asked to play more notes rather than change the tempo. Usually this means that they want you to play 'Double Time' which means that you need to change where you are putting the backbeat of your groove.

If that doesn't work then try adding more Ghost Notes into your groove or playing 16th notes on the Hi-Hats. This will give the impression that because there is more happening, the groove sounds 'faster'. If that still isn't working then play the snare drum slightly ahead of the beat! If one component of your groove is slightly ahead then it can add a feeling of 'urgency' to your groove. But don't play all the aspects of your groove ahead of the beat otherwise you'll just be speeding up. Play the Bass and Cymbals as you would normally, but play the Snare slightly earlier than normal.

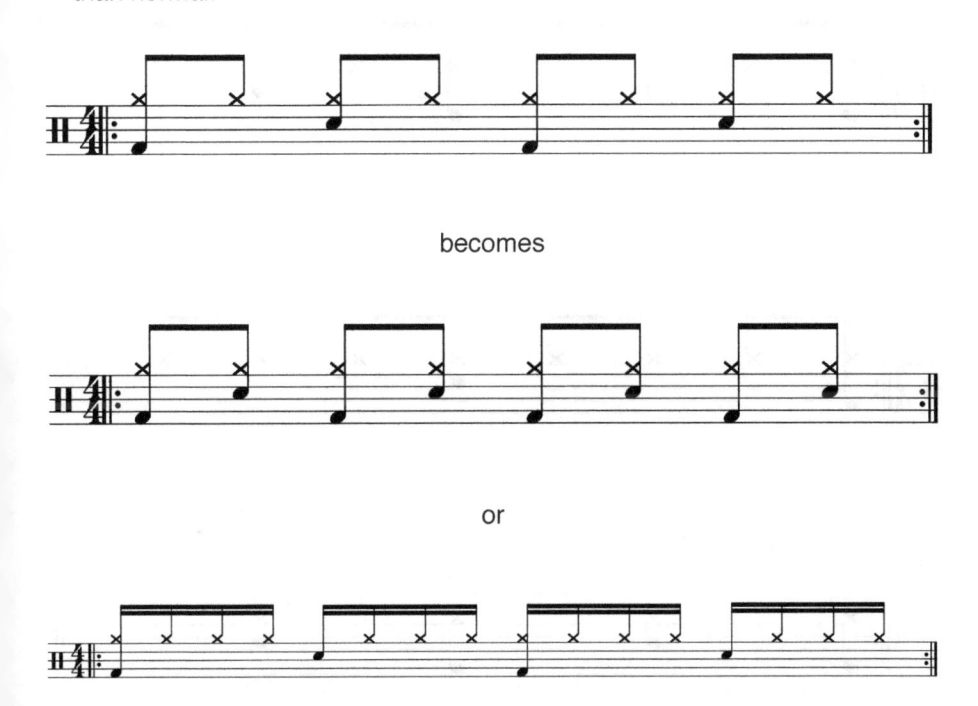

becomes

or

"SLOWER, BUT DO NOT SLOW DOWN!"

This has the same principle as the previous point, but you are most likely being asked to play a 'Half Time' groove. Basically play your backbeat on beat 3, instead of 2 and 4. This will give the illusion that the groove is slower without actually changing the tempo at all. Alternatively, you could play a groove as normal but delay the backbeat slightly so that the Snare comes a tiny bit late, which again can sound like you're playing slower when you're actually not.

Another potential option is to play fewer notes on the cymbals. So if you are playing 8th notes on your ride cymbal, try dropping to 1/4 but keeping the Bass and Snare parts the same. Less drums and more rest can usually give the space that the band actually want, even if they aren't asking for it directly.

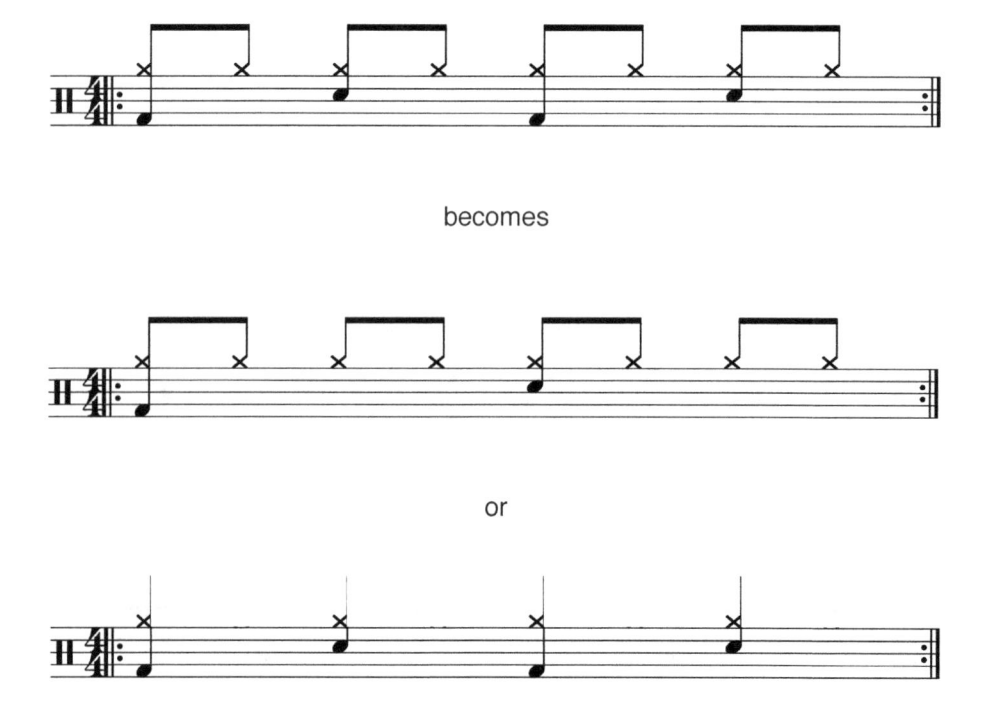

becomes

or

"MAKE IT SOUND BIGGER, BUT DONT PLAY LOUDER"

This is a case of thinking about WHERE you are playing on the kit instead of the VOLUME of which you are playing at. Instead of using your Hi-Hats, try using a Big Tom instead to add some depth and body to your groove. Or if that is too much then play on an open Hi-Hat instead of a closed one, or even on a Ride cymbal.

You need to think more about the dynamics of your playing as opposed to just hitting everything with more force. Try using the shoulder of the drumstick instead of the tip to find a deeper tone. It is about the sound coming from your kit, not necessarily the volume. In chapter 5 (In The Field) there is a section called '*The Art of Dynamic Playing*' which gives a lot more insight into this style of thinking and approach to playing this instrument. Helpful material when faced with these sorts of requests from your worship leader.

'RIM-CLICK' AND 'RIM-SHOT' ARE VERY DIFFERENT!

This mis-wording is so so so common and can have devastating results! To be honest it can actually be slightly hilarious... As drummers there are two ways of using the rim of the Snare drum. You can either strike the drum in the middle of the head whilst also hitting the rim with the shaft of the drumstick. What comes from this is a very loud 'crack' of a backbeat! This is called a Rim-shot. Alternatively, you can lay the stick down flat on the snare drum and use the butt of the stick to click the rim of the snare drum; which produces a lovely 'woodblock' sound. This is called a Rim-click.

These two words sound very similar but produce completely different sounds! When asked to play either of these, ALWAYS double check which version your worship leader is wanting. Just play one quickly and wait for the thumbs up. Nothing worse than a worship leader wanting a nice quiet vibe for a song, so they ask for a Rim-shot by accident so the drummer deafens the congregation with their thunder backbeat...

DRUM AND CYMBAL NAMES

It is pretty common for non-drummers to be unsure of the exact names of everything on your kit. This can lead to awkward situations where someone will ask you to play on something by giving it the completly wrong name. In some cases maybe even use phrases like "the really big thing" or "the one that's not the bass drum". If these kinds of phrases start coming at you then focus on the SOUND that they are asking for, not the specific name of the instrument.

If they want it louder, deeper, stronger, beefier, or more 'depthy' then they are probably asking for something like a Big Tom or a Bass Drum. If they are wanting something light, airy, pretty, subtle, washy, or 'pingy', then the cymbals are your best bet! The term 'washy' would work on a Crash, the term 'light' would work on a Ride cymbal and 'tight' would work on a closed Hi-Hat. It is all about taking what has been said and interpreting it into your language. Think about the sound, not always the exact name that has been given.

*

"A FIELD MANUAL;
BECAUSE IT NEEDS TO BE TAKEN INTO THE FIELD"

"WE ARE LEADING PEOPLE INTO AN ENCOUNTER WITH GOD. WE ARE NOT TRYING TO BLAST PEOPLE AWAY WITH OUR EXTENSIVE PLAYING"

TEN
WHO NEEDS WHAT

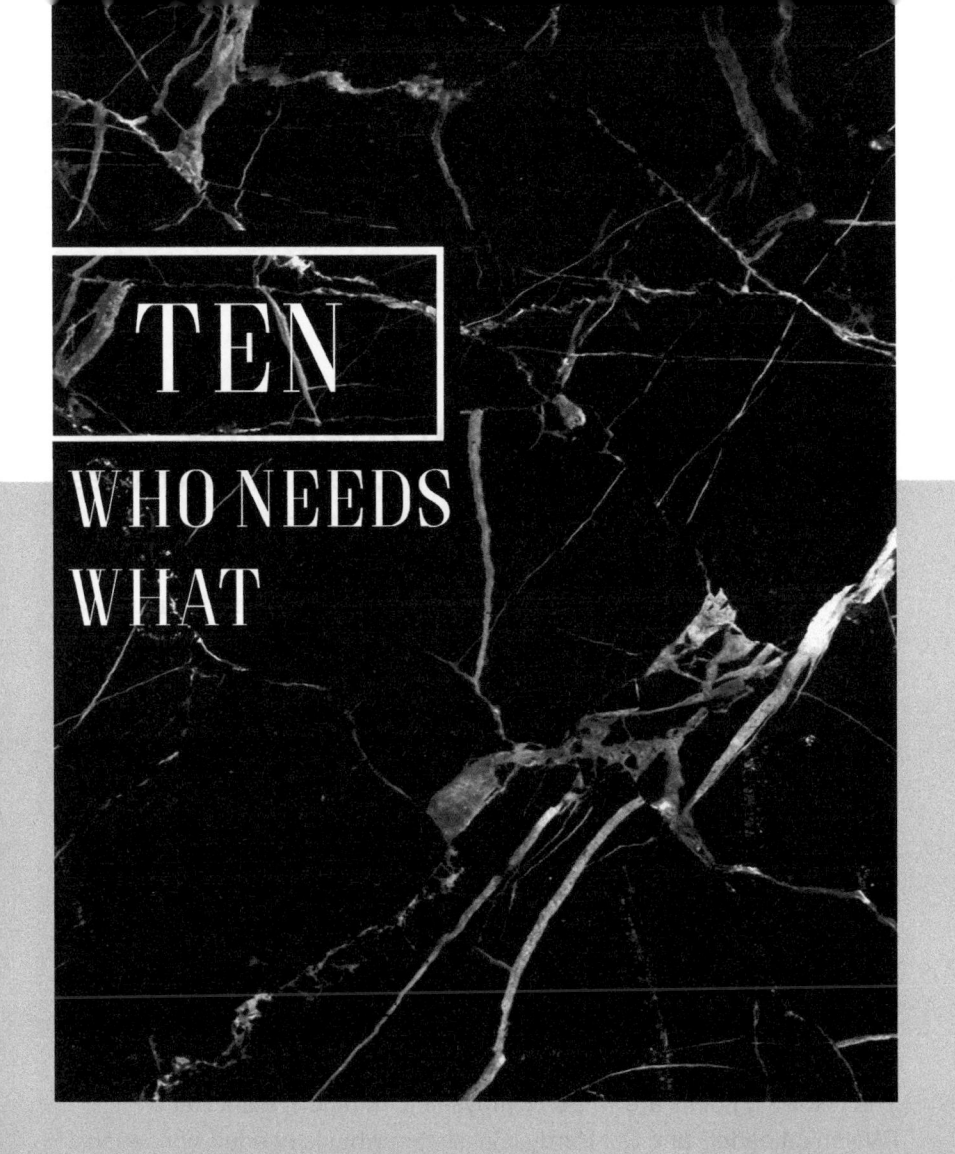

THE FIELD MANUAL

10
WHO NEEDS WHAT FROM WHO

What we as drummers can GIVE to others, and what we as drummers NEED from others.

This chapter was written with the purpose of being shared with a number of different people, not just drummers! It is a gift for making your worship team function smoothly and more cohesively. So please take this book, sit down with your worship leaders and read it together. There is useful information from both sides of the stage on what is needed from drummers, worship leaders, and bassists.

By some random event, if you are a Worship Leader who has accidentally picked up this book then please DO NOT put it down! If the drummer and worship leader can communicate and work together well then you will have a worship team to be reckoned with. So the insights given in this chapter could be really useful for you.

The following points are written by myself (Drummer), Mark Reid (Worship Leader) and Sol Hardy (Bassist) in what is needed from each other so that we can give our best to our worship bands and congregations. By gaining insight into each area of the band, the overall sound and dynamic of our music teams will increase. In the same way that a family understands each others needs, tendancies, and mannerisms, we need to be aware of what our fellow musicians are after and how we can work with them.
It's all super practical advice, so enjoy!

WHAT A DRUMMER NEEDS FROM THEIR WORSHIP LEADER

(AJ Rousell)

This section of the chapter is written directly to the Worship Leaders. Later in this chapter we will hear from a good friend of mine, and truly gifted worship leader, Mark Reid. But before we get to his input I am going to 'politely steal' a metaphor that he most likely 'politely stole' from someone else… (but it's my book, so there Reido!) He shared this analogy with me a few years ago and it really shaped my outlook on being the drummer in a Worship Team.

If we picture each member of a music team as a different section of a Cruise Ship (the SS Church Band) then the worship leader is the Captain and the drummer is everything mechancial that is found at the back of the ship. The general dynamic of each team is that the Worship Leader is the one who judges where a song should be heading and then communicates this with the band; the drummer is then the propeller and engine that actually makes it happen. This is because most musicians (maybe excluding guitarists…) will subconsciously follow the drums.

Creating a solid relationship with your drummer is an absolute must if you want your band to be effective at bringing your congregation into a worshipful place. Not understanding what your drummer needs will inevitably result in missed signals, misjudged changes, and confusion or friction whilst on stage.

But have no fear! The following 5 points were written by an actual drummer who can coherently highlight exactly what our funny breed of musician needs from their worship leader in order to function effectively:

1. THE HIGHWAY CODE ONLY WORKS WITH CLEAR SIGNALS; DRUMMERS ARE THE SAME

This sounds like an obvious point but it is surprising how the level of 'acceptable communication' can differ between each Worship Leader. Communication goes way beyond knowing which song is being played next or what the general 'vibe' required from the musicians is. There is nothing wrong with wanting to repeat a section or drop all the instruments out if that is what you feel needs to happen, but this needs to be expressed to your Drummer before it actually happens. There is nothing more awkward than when the Worship Leader just stops playing and the Drummer thunders on for another bar, completly unaware of your intent… Simple signals instantly let your Drummer know exactly what you are wanting to happen.

2. ALLOWING 'REACTION TIME' IS KEY FOR SMOOTH TRANSITIONS

So let's say you have a full list of signals that you and your drummer understand like the back of your hand. Brilliant! Now we need to highlight the on-stage etiquette needed to actually apply them effectively. 'Reaction Time' (RT) is essentially the space between receiving a clear signal and then executing the requested musical change. Many worship leaders do not fully grasp that RT is the key factor in controlling how smooth a transition is within a song.

As an example, let us visualise a situation in which the worship leader would like the whole band to drop out for a section. The amount of RT given to the drummer dictates whether that dynamic change is musically smooth, or a sudden jolt into awkward silence. Allocating a RT of one or two full bars can give your drummer enough space to musically lead the band and congregation into any change using appropriate drum fills or a change of groove. This is so much more pleasing to the ear and also keeps all of your musicians on the same page.

3. WHETHER A DECISION WAS RIGHT OR WRONG, YOU NEED TO STAND BY IT

One of the worst things that a Worship Leader can do is either shyly creep into a section, or fall into a melody halfway through the lyric. Confidence is everything when leading a worship team, and the byproduct of this is the necessity of fully committing to a decision. Regardless of whether it could be considered right or wrong, it is always better to make a judgement and then stick to it. If your Drummer is listening and responsive then they will always adjust to what they see you doing, resulting in the rest of the band following in the same direction. Uncertainty and doubt can be damagingly contagious in a musical group so needs to be avoided at all costs.

4. BE GRACIOUS WHEN YOUR DRUMMER COUNTS IN

As drummers, there is a strong chance that we have played with multiple worship leaders in a variety of bands. A lot of worship leaders don't realise that everyone has an "inner-clock' that lets us all know whether a song is too fast, too slow or just right. The tricky thing about this is that every worship leaders inner-clock is slightly different. So be gracious with your drummer because even though they know the song and structure, there is a strong chance that when they played the song with a different worship leader the tempo was different to how you like it. Sometimes they just won't count it in with the tempo that YOU feel the track sounds best at, so encourage them to speed it up or slow down within the intro and then the rest of the track should run smoothly.

4. LEARN THE TECHNICAL TERMS FOR WHAT YOU WOULD LIKE YOUR DRUMMER TO PLAY

Now I am not denying that this can sometimes be impossible to do! If you eavesdrop on Drummers that are deep in conversation then there is a chance you will hear words such as Paradiddles, Patta-fla-fla's, Flams, Vic Firth, or double stroke rolls… Total gibberish to the non-drummer! So what practical phrases are good to know when trying to communicate with your Drummer?

The individual names of each component on the drum kit is a great start. *"Can you add more Bass Drum to that beat"* versus *"Can you hit the really big one more than you're hitting the flat metal things"* can save so much time in establishing a mutual understanding. You can push this idea even further by familiarising yourself with the names of various subdivisions that you would like your Drummer to use. Asking your Drummer to play 16th notes on the Hi-Hat Cymbal will usually be met with an immediate understanding of what you are after (1/4 Notes, 8th notes, 16th Notes, and Triplets are the main four to know). This takes a lot less time compared to using A Capella to sing the desired drum beat…

5. POSITIVITY AND NEGATIVITY ARE BOTH CONTAGIOUS

This point could be considered just "fishing for compliments", but it really isn't. Encouragement is something that is strongly promoted in the Bible, so it has to be applied to all the musicians you are working with. Drummers that want to give their absolute best can be a very self-critical bunch, therefore if nothing is said to them after a service then they will contemplate and analyse whether their playing was up to scratch. A simple thank you or encouraging word on an aspect of their playing (even if you have to really search for one) can work wonders. A simple but golden concept! It is no secret that there are countless numbers of 'Drummer Jokes' floating around on the internet, and although the majority of Drummers will take these with a pinch of salt, some may allow this stereotype to affect their mindset. 'Pretend Musicians' and the Cadbury Gorilla are all recognisable images, so verbally highlighting to your Drummer the importance of their instrument gives them a role within the team, which can be an incredibly valuable and engaging tool.

*

WHAT A WORSHIP LEADER NEEDS FROM THEIR DRUMMER

(Mark Reid)

One of my dearest friends, Mark Reid, has kindly agreed to shed some light on what a Worship Leader needs and desires from their drummer. What is it that makes a Worship Leader want to work with, and enjoy playing with a drummer. Mark is an incredibly gifted Worship Leader who I have spent years playing with, in various situations and capacities. We both understand how the other ticks and how we can serve each other whilst leading worship.

He is truly anointed as a Worship Leader, so it is a real privilege to have him share some insight on this subject. As drummers, if we are aware of what our Worship Leaders are trying to capture and how they are wanting their musicians to assist them in that, then we are on a sure line to creating a musically pleasant, worship filled atmosphere.
Side note; reading the following points in a smooth Irish accent really helps. Here is what Mark had to say:

1. HOW'S YOUR HEART?
This is an important thing to reflect on before we move anywhere. Before you are a drummer you are a person. A person who is completely loved by God and in response wants to love Him back. The job of the worship team on a Sunday is to lead people into an encounter with God using music as the tool. So, the grooves that the drummer plays should be a simple overflow of how they should try to live their life.

Ray Hughes is a musician who I greatly admire. He carries an enormous amount of wisdom around worship and says this: "When we create, God simply reveals another facet of his nature." So, every time a drummer hits the snare or the bell of the ride as an expression of praise, there is a chance for God to reveal another element of who he is.

What's my point? Worship is prophetic and I believe musicians are to be a prophetic people. If the people of God are gathered in Church to encounter God, and we as the musicians are holding a tool that may help them encounter God, then we need to be a prophetic people who are listening to the promptings of the Spirit.

That is what I'm doing every time I get up to lead, and I want the musicians I play with to be doing the same. To be a prophetic people, we primarily need to be lovers of God. So before anything, when I'm leading worship and my drummer turns up, I want him or her to be a lover of God who wants to hear His voice.

2. SIMPLER IS USUALLY BETTER

Before I started to lead worship, I played drums. I was the drummer in my home church in Ireland. Even in my current church in Bristol I played drums before I started leading. So I recognise that sometimes the big fills and Gospel chops are very tempting when playing a standard 4/4 groove at 60BPM.

However, we need to look at the bigger picture. We are leading people into an encounter with God. We are not trying to blast people away with our extensive playing. We must remember that in our playing we are serving. We're serving God, we're serving the congregation, and we're serving the song. Playing a complicated groove over a mid-tempo 6/8 song can be really unhelpful.

So when I'm leading, I want my drummer to be playing appropriate grooves and fills rather than trying to impress everyone with some technically incredible groove.

3. ARE YOU FAT?

I remember when I was younger, my mum gave me a challenge that completely re-shaped my view on playing music in a worship context. She said: "Mark! Are you FAT?". Sure, when I first heard that I was shocked and even a little offended. But she unpacked the question with me and asked if I was a person who was (and still is) FAITHFUL, AVAILABLE and TEACHABLE. (F.A.T)

The faithful element goes back to my opening point about the heart, the availability element speaks about how "up for it" you are, and the teachable element is about our willingness to learn and develop.

When I lead, I want my drummer to be willing to receive feedback. Feedback helps us grow, and challenges us, and even causes us to discern if we don't fully agree with it. It's always such a joy to have a drummer come up to you and ask you for feedback on their playing. It displays a heart that wants to learn.

4. HEAD UP!

Eye contact is key! A lot of the musical worship in Churches can be led from the acoustic guitar. This means that the acoustic guitar may be the instrument setting the rhythm and the tempo of a song. So, keep your head up, always be looking at the worship leader and be responsive to where they may take a song next!

5. BE SENSITIVE

Sensitivity is key in a worship context. People are looking for an encounter with God and don't want your playing to get in the way of that! Be aware of what is going on in the room. Does your playing facilitate or hinder what the Lord is doing?

WHAT A BASSIST NEEDS FROM THEIR DRUMMER

(Sol Hardy)

It was written earlier on in this book about the importance of the rhythm section in any band being tight and working together. It is the core of the music group that the other instruments rest on, so if it isn't sounding unified then the end result is a lot of mess. So it is no surprise that it is very important to really understand what our partners in rhythm need from us as drummers. I feel very fortunate that this next section was written by one of my closest friends and favourite bass players, Sol Hardy.

Sol and I lived together while studying music, and since then we have played together in countless churches and have worked with each other professionally for a number of years. Sol and I have gigged in some of the most enjoyable environments, and also shared some of the worst gigs of our careers together. So our experience of working together as a rhythm section is seasoned and tested.

When asking what his fellow bassists need from their drummers, there were some great pearls of wisdom. Here is what Sol had to say:

1. LEARN TO HAVE A SOLID GROOVE AND STICK TO IT!
It's really hard for a bass player to enjoy the groove and try and be creative when the bass drum pattern is constantly changing! Choose a groove and sit with it through the different sections of the song unless you have to change it. This means we as bassists have something reliable to work with.

2. KNOW THE POINT OF YOUR INSTRUMENT AND WHERE IT FITS WITHIN MUSIC

It's very common to be able to play an instrument before you understand where the instrument sits in its frequencies. It is so important in making the overall sound not become too messy, and the art is learning how to spread the musical load evenly around the stage.
As bass players, we know that we are in the lower end of the spectrum of music and frequencies. So if we are playing with lots of middle and treble instruments (for example guitars and vocals) we know there is a lot of room to be creative in the lower notes of the bass. You could argue this as overplaying, but I like to call it understanding sound and knowing where the space is for more movement.

There is a strong chance we are playing with a drummer that uses lots of kick drum, big toms, and sub drop samples. Plus there may also be a synth player or pianist! Everyone needs to be aware of ALL the frequencies happening onstage. If everyone is smacking the low-end frequencies, we might need to ease up and play something quite straight. If not it can be far too messy with not enough clarity (this is the point in the service where someone will inevitably complain about "noise"…)

For drummers, I think this is something that is overlooked and is key to our overall worship sound. Be aware that lots of people are singing and trying to connect, so smashing on cymbals that are around the same frequency will not help the overall sound. Learn this and you may start finding a real love for dynamic playing that locks in with your bass player, not just another boring paradiddle-based cymbal embellishment.

3. USE YOUR EARS!

As a bass player, my job is to tie the melody with the rhythm. Practically that can involve changing the root note when the chords change whilst also locking in with the drummer as best I can.

However, in a lot of church contexts you could be playing a song where the chords are changing on the 1st and 3rd beat of the bar, yet the drummer's kick pattern is emphasising the offbeats or the 'e' or 'a' of a beat (16th Notes).

Even though you can make this work as a bassist, the rhythm and melody aren't completely tied together so it makes our lives much harder and affects the overall 'tightness' of a band. As drummers, still be listening to the other instruments so as a rhythm section we can lock everything together.

4. ALWAYS BE MUSICALLY MINDED

Just because the original song might have a really cool fill or a slightly quirky groove, doesn't mean it is always helpful for people responding in your church context. Sometimes the original song may have been played to a stadium-sized congregation, with a click, with a 16 piece backing band, which just simply won't work in your home church.

You don't always have to play that stuff exactly like the track, so instead think about how your playing is going to impact the room you are in. If your creativity helps then go for it loud and proud, but if not then hold it back for your function gigs or other bands…

5. BUILD RELATIONSHIPS WITH THE BAND, ESPECIALLY THE WORSHIP LEADER

I always want to know where the worship leader likes to go musically, or their intent behind their decisions. It's not wrong to talk about practical things or what people like. You are all individuals and creating one unified sound in a short practice is not easy.

So be communicative by chatting with the bassist about what they like and how they play.

Decide who's going to create the groove and who's going to follow. Communicate when you're thinking of dynamically building up or dropping down so the bassist is also on board and creates those dynamic changes with you.

6. STOP PRACTICING DRUM FILLS WHEN YOU GET ON THE KIT!!
Tune your kit, then either stop noodling or start practicing a groove that I can lock in with!

*

"ONE OF THE MOST **BEAUTIFUL THINGS** ABOUT THE CHURCH IS THE DIVERSITY OF THEIR CONGREGATIONS!"

ELEVEN
REMOVING L PLATES

THE FIELD
MANUAL

11

REMOVING THE 'L' PLATES
DEVELOPING, EDUCATING, AND ENCOURAGING

Church worship teams are varied in many ways. This includes the characters within each team, the level of musicianship, the professions of each member, the length of time they have been a Christian, and their background or upbringing. One of the most beautiful things about the Church is the diversity of their congregations! Whilst it is a beautiful element it can obviously come with its complications and difficulties.

One common frustration and difficulty is when you have a group of musicians working together, but the level of musicianship is as diverse as their characteristics. This chapter looks at two main categories; Firstly, how we as drummers should approach playing with musicians who are new to their instrument. Secondly, how existing team members can approach bringing new musicians into their worship groups and equipping them in their role. This chapter looks at both aspects:

PLAYING WITH BEGINNER MUSICIANS

This is a big deal. It's tricky to ask ourselves this question without immediately feeling cocky or arrogant, but it is sometimes just the reality. What do we do when the musicians we are playing with aren't as practiced as we are? This is something that can lead to a really challenging situation for some musicians. The skill level of musicians around all the churches are as varied as the Church itself. Some musicians are hobby musicians, some are professional, some used to be professional, some are self-taught, and some have only started learning because their church was missing that specific instrument!

The following section is written for the experienced and able drummers who are serving in their churches. It surrounds the concept of what to do when you find yourself playing in a Worship Team with polar opposite skill levels. It can appear like a boastful, self-elevating attitude to have, but what the next few points will show is actually how different your reaction should be in this situation.

ADJUST YOUR PLAYING, NOT THEIRS!

"Be completely humble and gentle; be patient, bearing with one another in love" (Ephesians 4:2) A big concept but a super valuable one! When we are playing with musicians who aren't as practiced or experienced, the best reaction you can have is to adjust your playing to accommodate them. Do not force it to work the other way around! Humility is such an appealing characteristic, especially in musicians. If you are playing with musicians with minimal experience, then you need to become their support. Shift your thinking from what you would ideally like to play, and think about what the other musicians need in order to make the band AS A WHOLE sound good.

If your bass player is new to the instrument, consider how complicated you kick drum pattern is. If your singer lacks confidence, be aware how complicated your groove is and how easy it is to sync up with. If a musician in the band has inconsistent timing, make sure your Hi-Hat or Snare is slightly louder so there is a clear and solid pulse for them to cling to. Or, if a guitarist is struggling with the timing of a riff, be aware that your job will be to keep the rest of the band in time, so make the downbeat super obvious!

This is all part of being aware and observant as drummers, which results in us being able to look after the band as a whole, not just ourselves and the bass player.

BE THE FOUNDATION

'The loftier the building, the deeper the foundation must be laid'
(Thomas a Kemper)

Our role as drummers can become exceptionally obvious and important when we find ourselves in this situation. We have read countless times that the drummer is the rock and foundation of a band, but it is easy to be a foundation when the building isn't in an earthquake... When you have a mixed bag of musicians in a music team it has the potential to be a brilliant learning curve, but also carries the potential to be a turbulent experience. This is where our role as drummers becomes crucial!

As I said before, a foundation has a fairly stress-free job when a building is in a calm and stress-free environment. It is when the structural integrity of a building becomes unstable due to a stressful environment that the importance of its foundation becomes critical. We need to have this mindset as drummers! When the atmosphere is difficult and the fluidity of musicianship isn't comfortable, it becomes our job to get everyone on the same page. Being clear and concise in how we explain, demonstrate, and request ideas is key.

It is important to realise that the language we use to communicate with other musicians can have a really powerful effect on how well it is received. If you are playing with musicians that haven't had as much instrumental education, avoid using technical jargon and too many "musician-y" terms. Rest assured that this isn't patronising or condescending because it is simply meeting them where they are at and communicating in ways that will benefit both parties.

The trick is not to be obvious that you are avoiding technical terms! Sometimes, in order to get the best from a group, there needs to be a lot of 'self-humbling'. This can also be healthy for keeping ourselves respectfully grounded as musicians. As a drummer who has worked hard and practiced you are there to teach, inspire, demonstrate and encourage.

RAISING UP NEW MUSICIANS

Churches are forever in need of musicians for their worship teams. Bringing new musicians into the team is a great start, but building them up and developing their skills is where the life of the church really comes into its own. As drummers that have played in Church for a while, we sometimes find ourselves in the situation where a newer drummer has shown an interest and needs some guidance. This is a really special opportunity to impart experience and advice as we raise up another drummer.

Competitiveness within musical environments is something that can be naturally present, but can also be toxic. You can't be competitive when it comes to art, so try and avoid feeling that another drummer is 'on your turf'. We are all in this game together. Raising up the next generation of church drummers can be a real privilege. Here are some thoughts:

THE INFLUENCE OF HAVING A ROLE

A while ago I heard a really interesting comment surrounding the idea of keeping people in the church, but sadly can't remember where or who I heard it from. They said that for an individual to want to stay in a church they sometimes need to **Belong** before they **Believe**. This was talking more about individuals who are not yet Christians, but elements of this point can still carry some value when discussing raising up new musicians in your church bands.

Juust to clarify, I do believe that the spiritual walk that our musicians are on is really important. For a musician to truly understand what is needed of them, they need to first engage with their own worship. The aspect of my mysterious quote is specifically the idea of 'having a role'. In the first chapter, we looked at the importance of rhythm in music and the power that music carries. When bringing new musicians into your team this can be a really useful tool to bear in mind.

For people to want to remain serving, they need to feel engaged with their role. Being reminded of the importance of their instrument or job is the starting point for bringing new musicians into the fold and gives them a sense of belonging. It is from there that we can equip, educate, and empower those individuals because they are aware of how crucial their role can be when it is done well! Frequently remind them that what they are bringing is so key to the overall sound and dynamic.

FROM THE GROUND UP

So many of the UK's cities have amazing music scenes that are thriving and producing phenomenal musicians. It is exceptionally rare though for an established musician to become 'well-known' without doing a lot of groundwork. For a musician to become connected with other musicians, and be regularly called upon, requires spending a large amount of time meeting people and playing with as many musicians as possible. It can sometimes be the same in Church, but in other cases it is exactly the opposite. Some churches have no choice but to throw their musicians in at the deep end. There can still be real value in starting your new musician's journey from humble beginnings.

Start them small! Sometimes it's ok to avoid the 'thrown in the deep end' situations if possible. Bring them into the group by accompanying an already established musician. For example, playing percussion with the main drummer, playing alongside another guitarist, or co-leading one of the songs in the service. Although, sometimes this can only come from the luxury of having a large number of musicians in your team. If you have one drummer who has come forward as keen and available, then the decision not to throw them straight in may be out of your hands. But if there is the opportunity to develop them from the ground-up, it can have much better results in the long run.

In a church that holds multiple services, there is real value in starting a musician out by playing the smaller services. This can be good for various reasons which include developing confidence and experience. Yet within all of this, it can install a servant heart into a musician which is invaluable. So often we can fall into the trap of running after the big service with the huge congregation and spectacular lights! Yet the smaller and more intimate service is still where God can spectacularly move, so being able and willing to do both really shows a musician's motives and heart. Humble beginnings can be so important in the overall growth of our music teams.

'LUCK' IS WHAT HAPPENS WHEN PREPARATION MEETS OPPORTUNITY

A **calling** instigates a need to prepare, and **preparation** usually requires education, and **education** usually involves **investing**.
This is a conversation that many church leaders have shared experience on and it really carries some insightful ideas. What happens when someone approaches a leader and says, "I feel a strong calling to preach/lead/play", but (to put it plainly) their abilities to do so are seriously lacking. It can sound judgmental and condescending to say that, but sometimes that is just the reality.

This is a moment that can either smash someone's dream or inspire them to go for it full throttle. The big question; "What have you been doing to prepare for that Calling?"

This applies to all aspects of our lives. Just because we feel God is calling us into something, doesn't mean that it will then require no effort from us. Sometimes we hear the call way ahead of when that calling will actually be birthed to life. There is so much importance in hearing a call from the Father and then being ready for when the opportunity finally presents itself.

If you feel a call to preach, but don't have the opportunity, start writing sermons and studying communicative practices. If you feel a call to lead a Church but can't find the opportunity, work alongside existing pastors and study the world's great leaders. If you feel a call to play an instrument in your Church worship team but can't find the opportunity, start preparing and practicng for it now! Have lessons with experienced drummers, save money, buy decent equipment, practice as much as you can, and watch and study worship sessions. Be serious about your calling and get good at what you feel you are being called to be doing in the future!

"Luck" is what happens when preparation meets opportunity. Whatever that calling is, honour it by investing in it and preparing for it. When wanting to bring new musicians into a team, it is ok to give this advice to those who have the heart for worship but haven't invested in the skills required. If done well it can give the inspiration and motivation they need to practice and step into their calling when they are ready.

ENCOURAGEMENT WHEN CORRECTING

"The mediocre teacher tells. The good teacher explains. The superior teacher demonstrates. The great teacher inspires."
(William Arthur Ward.)

There is a balance between encouragement and correction. One without the other can have damagingly negative effects. If a musician's attitude or playing has noticeable complications, and yet they only receive praise and compliments, there is potential for a self-involved, vain musician to develop. On the other hand, if a musician only hears feedback when mistakes are made, there is greater potential for a lack of confidence or lessened self-worth. It is a really tricky tightrope to balance on…

The main thing to consider is that it is ok to correct, it is ok to advise, and it is ok to give constructive feedback. But this only really carries any weight when the positives are also highlighted. So often it can be easy to forget to praise when a service goes well, and only bring to light the areas that were not great. Both encouragement and correction go hand in hand when bringing new musicians into a team or equipping the existing ones. It is a case of not giving false praise, whilst also not only correcting the mistakes.

A practical concept that comes with experience, prayer, and wisdom.

*

"IT'S A FUNNY CONCEPT WHEN YOU THINK ABOUT; WORSHIPPING THROUGH HITTING SOMETHING WITH A STICK."

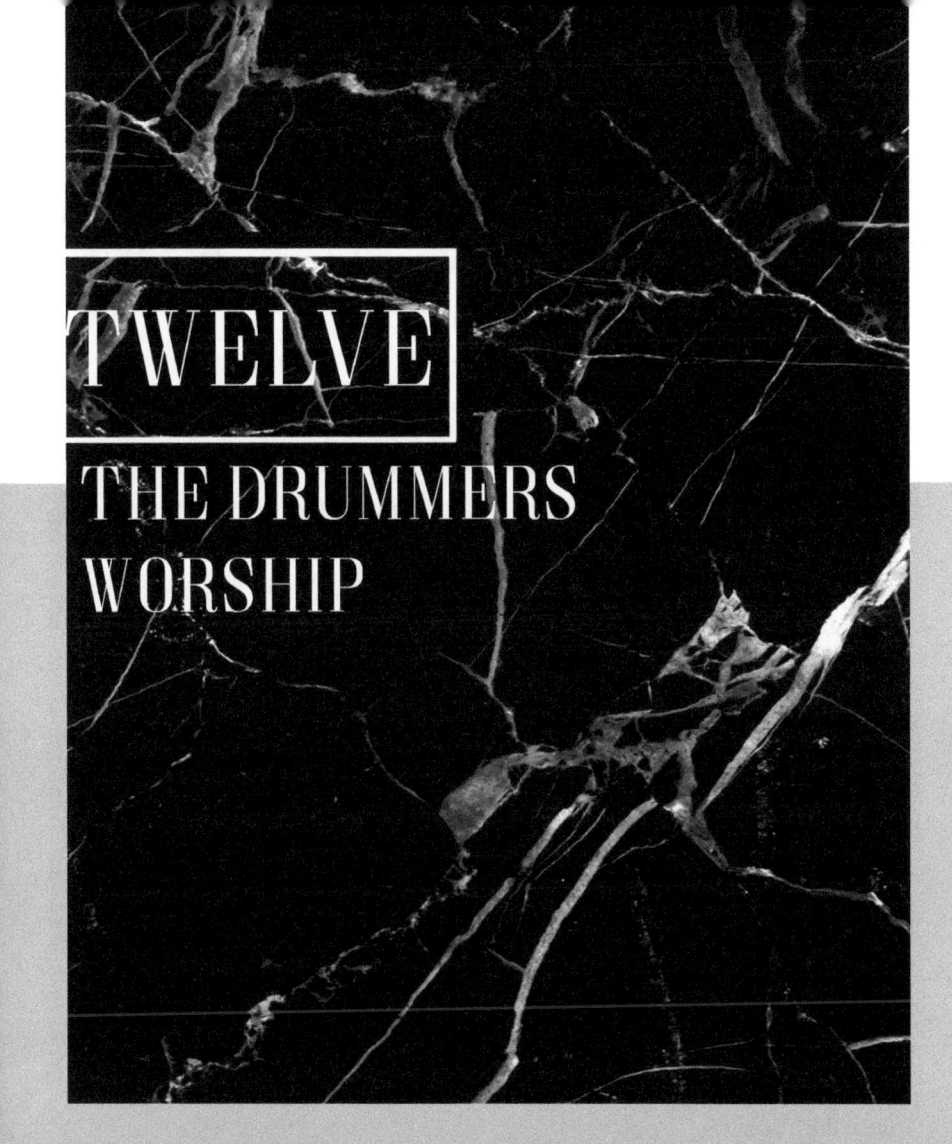

TWELVE
THE DRUMMERS WORSHIP

THE FIELD MANUAL

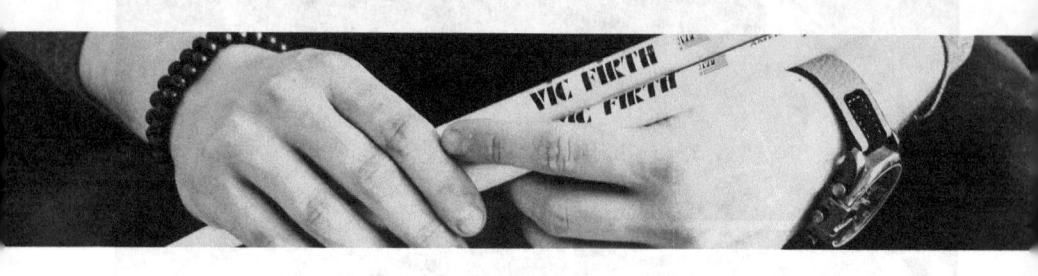

12

THE DRUMMER'S WORSHIP

"Your talent is God's gift to you, how you use it is your gift back to God." (Leo Buscaglia)

There has been a large amount of practical information in this book that has covered a wide range of drumming, musical, and personal aspects of our lives as church drummers. We have spent a large proportion of these chapters looking at how to "give our best" to our churches and to survive and thrive in various musical settings. Like many things in life, we can expect to save the most important information until the end. That is exactly why this chapter is here.

The practical information is so important and can really help with how to deliver the musical elements of our role as drummers, but at the end of the day it is all irrelevant if the heart behind what we are doing isn't focussed on the right thing. We are first called to be worshippers, and from that place we lead other people in worship. If we find our validation and identity in our label and role, then we are inevitably preparing for a heap of trouble!

I love being a drummer, I literally love it, and at the time of writing this book there is honestly nothing I would rather be doing than working as a professional musician. BUT, what would happen to my mental well-being and 'soul-spark' if that was all taken away for reasons that were out of my control? I remember reading an interview with a well-known drummer who played in an incredibly established band that were regularly selling out stadiums with a number of well-received albums. Sadly, this drummer developed an illness that resulted in his limbs not functioning as they used to, which meant that drumming eventually became impossible for him. Listening to his story of how he spiralled into depression and suicidal thoughts really struck a chord with me. If we find our self-worth, value, and identity in earthly roles and physical concepts then we are losing sight of what is important. This has been a real challenge for me and results in a daily prayer to re-align my thoughts on God, not my instrument or career. A prayer (which I still find difficult to pray sometimes) is simply "Father help me to not seek validation from my peers or strangers, give me confidence that you have put me where I am meant to be, and I will choose to rejoice in that. First and foremost, I am your kid, everything else is just a bonus". It's tough stuff, but it's so beneficial and you will view your playing and involvement in your church differently because of it.

Having mentioned the idea that all the practical information is irrelevant unless the heart behind it is right, how then does that look? As Christians we are called to Worship, and because of that we have an opportunity to contribute as drummers. It needs to be that way around to really connect with what we are doing as drummers who are leading worship. It is impossible to write these paragraphs without sharing some personal experiences and struggles.

Vulnerability is always fun (rolls eyes) and that is what I have had to really push during this chapter. There have been personal struggles along my musical and worshipful journey, and I am hoping that by highlighting and explaining the process of pushing past them it will help other musicians with their own worship. So, a lot of this chapter is personal reflections. I'm sorry (also not sorry) for the number of I's, Me's and Mine's you are about to read…

There are a few things to think about when contemplating these ideas:

THE DIFFERENCE BETWEEN BEING IN A WORSHIP BAND, AND BEING A WORSHIPPER

Serving in a worship band can be incredibly fun as it gives us a chance to play our instrument with other musicians. As drummers we have an added blessing; we never have to look for a seat in a church as there is already one there for us! The music team is a great place to serve, but can also lead to a not-so-great reflex... When watching a vast number of interviews with well-known musicians, the question of how they got into music is a commonly asked one. The common response is that the musician had negative emotions, experiences, or situations that music provided an escape from. Locked away from the world that was hurting them they found comfort, peace, and distraction from reality. Although not as extreme, it is possible for a similar scenario to happen to our worship teams. Music can easily become a distraction from our reality.

Speaking personally, I spent years being involved in various worship teams while having no desire or apparent ability to actually worship. I was very busy and was usually playing in a music team every week, which in hindsight was a distraction from the reality that I simply didn't enjoy worship and had no desire to connect with God. Playing the drums once a week meant that I was INVOLVED in worship, but was not ACTIVELY worshipping. **It is one thing to be a drummer in a worship band, it is another thing altogether to be a worshipper that plays drums.**

"The Lord says: "These people come near to me with their mouth and honour me with their lips, but their hearts are far from me. Their worship of me is based on merely human rules they have been taught. (Isaiah 29:13). The willingness of our spirits, and openness of our hearts are the contributing factors to whether we are using drumming as a form of escapism.

It is something to be aware of and to regularly come back and check on. It is ok to occasionally ask to not play one week if you feel that you actually just need some genuine worship time. Genuine worship time, as in where you are fully focussing on God with no distractions of musicality or awareness of your role as a drummer. This leads nicely into the following paragraphs about how that actually looks…

IT SHOULDN'T MATTER WHERE YOU ARE IN THE ROOM

This concept is a really challenging one and can be a genuine struggle for some. Here are questions that have frequently come to mind:
Does it matter that you are on stage when you are worshipping? Do people only worship on stage because they are aware they are on show? What if people think I'm trying to "look super holy" if I worship on stage? How can I ignore that I am essentially worshipping in front of X amount of people? How do I stop that feeling that my worship could be becoming a 'Performance'? Are people observing how I worship? What are people thinking if/when they see me worshipping?

All these questions can become easy to start wrestling with and potentially a real struggle to push past. We are involved in a team within the church that spends a large percentage of its time in front of a congregation. Sometimes on a stage and sometimes even on cameras! It can be so easy to become over-aware and self-conscious, not in our playing but in our worshipping. Many drummers will happily play in front of thousands of people with lights and cameras lighting them up, but worshipping (which is something that can be so personal and intimate) in front of 30 people can carry a completely different feeling.

There was a very persistent lie that I believed for years that I feel needs to be mentioned to guide other musicians away from it; "If I worship whilst on stage people will assume I am only worshippin BECAUSE I am on stage…"

This lie resulted in me being unable to worship whilst on a stage due to a fear of judgement or being labeled 'showy'. So, I would rather sit on the kit and stare at the floor than give the impression I was trying to look super-holy or get more screen time because my hands were up. It has been a real process that has given many lessons and revelations. One consideration for pushing into how we worship is to look at the three different worship settings and how they all intertwine:

1. PERSONAL WORSHIP

This is where everything begins and yet can sometimes be the hardest to engage with. This is the alone time where we search more for God and try to discover more of him. It is our day to day living that also mixes in with our desire to walk closer with God in everything we do.

Personally, I really struggle to engage that quiet time and sit with God, it almost feels like something that just doesn't come naturally. But, in the same way that musicians practice what we can't play to better ourselves, it is ok to practice spending time with God to find what works for us and what doesn't.

How we are when we are alone with God is what will then be reflected in our works, character, and worship. I'm always drawn to Jesus's word, *"And when you pray, do not be like the hypocrites, for they love to pray standing in the synagogues and on the street corners to be seen by others. Truly I tell you, they have received their reward in full."* (Matthew 6:5)

Although this message is so applicable for how we worship, it can easily be taken to an unhealthy extreme where we only worship when we are alone and out of sight. This smoothly leads onto another style of worship…

2. COMMUNAL WORSHIP

Every day they continued to meet together in the temple courts. They broke bread in their homes and ate together with glad and sincere hearts, praising God and enjoying the favour of all the people. And the Lord added to their number daily those who were being saved. (Acts 2:46-47)

'Community' is a very commonly used word within church contexts; it is something that I had a really negative view of for a number of years after experiencing a bad representation of it. When community is done properly it is incredible and can add so much to our lives. This transcends into when we worship communally. There is something very unique about when a group of individuals come together and are unified in who they are worshipping; which is something to embrace, not run from. It can be tricky though when there are other people involved. Self-consciousness, over-awareness of others, and distractions from peers can all become a factor in these situations which can hinder us from worshipping. These are all natural human sesponses but are also reactions that need to be turned away from with intent and thought.

The Psalms give a verse that is perfect, *"I will tell of your name to my brothers; in the midst of the congregation I will praise you."* (Psalm 22:22). It shows the importance of worship within a communal setting and shows that worship is something we also choose to do. Sometimes it is a choice that we have to chase after, ignoring all our natural human reactions and pushing aside our awareness of exterior factors.

This can especially be applied when it comes to being in a congregation, while another band is leading worship. We are musicians, therefore we will notice mistakes and we will be observing everything that is happening musically. In many cases, we do it without even realising we are doing it! The challenge here is to hold it as just that; an observation. As soon as our observations build barriers within our worship then we are missing the point of why we are there.

It is so easy to fall into 'musical snobbery' and become unable to worship unless the musicians playing are audibly and visually pleasing to us.

Again, this is a natural human reaction that needs to be pushed aside as we choose to worship, despite what is happening in front of us. In an attempt not to make a brash and heavily intense comment; God is big enough to see past our sin, so we need to become big enough to see past our musical observations. Having looked at the previous two worship settings, there is a third that wraps this whole process up nicely with a bow on top.

3. THE "YOU-JUST-HAPPEN-TO-BE-ON-STAGE" WORSHIP

For me, this situation has been a real battle to work through. One solid conclusion is that it is nearly impossible to completely switch off from the fact that you are in front of a room full of people. If someone opens their eyes and looks forward, there you are. Now, the majority of people won't even acknowledge you are there or what you are doing, and if that is the case then it shows that you are doing your job well as a worship band. But those insecurities can still be present…

A big fear of mine was that everything I did was to self-glorify or give a false image of "holiness". My fear of being perceived as a "show off worshipper" became bigger than my desire to genuinely worship. It is unhealthy and spiritually draining to suppress those feelings whilst constantly rationalising about what others may or may not be thinking. A conclusion I have come to is a simple question that I ask myself while leading worship with a team; *"Would I, and do I, worship like this when I'm not on stage?"* If the answer to that question is a genuine, honest, and sincere 'YES' then crack on!

Our worship should be consistent and regular, irrelevant of whereabouts in the building we are stood (or sat). How we worship in the personal quiet place should reflect how we worship in the communal setting, which in turn is a mirror of how we worship when on stage. They are all the same! Worship should not be considered an action that is dictated by situational or environmental factors. We are born worshippers, regardless of where that takes place. When we play in a worship band we are praising through our instrument, which comes from deep place within ourselves, which is shaped in the personal and communal space.

"Praise him with the sounding of trumpets, praise him with the harp and lyre, praise him with timbrel and dancing, praise him with the strings and pipe, praise him with the clash of cymbals, praise him with resounding cymbals." (Psalm 150: 3-5)

THE STORY BEHIND CHAPTER 3

Early in this book we explored a chapter titled "Giving Your Best". It looked into how we as drummers should be developing attitudes of not just giving half an effort, and offering the best of ourselves as a sign of worship. The chapter opened with the mental, biblical, and spiritual aspects of carrying that attitude, but the story behind that revelation wasn't a pleasant one. For that reason, it didn't seem appropriate to introduce the chapter with it, but it also doesn't feel like something to be ignored. It is a testimony of when God conducted himself as a disciplinary father figure, something that none of us like to acknowledge. Yet regardless of our uncomfortableness, his discipline is truly loving, and this story is a testament to that.

So, let's travel back in time; I'm about 22 years old and pursuing drumming as a career. I was studying a BA Hons in Professional Musicianship at university, playing in seemingly every band under the sun, and meeting as many musicians as I possibly could. Alongside this, I was playing in my church and had really established myself as a regularly called upon drummer. Everything was going great except for my faith, spiritual satisfaction, and emotional well-being. It was one of those times that many find themselves in where the personal stuff just wasn't going that well. To put it plainly, my lifestyle outside of the church was simply not matching how I was within the church. What had become my 'normality' was being regularly inconsiderate of how my Saturday night might affect my Sunday morning.

So yet again, it's 8:15am and I had found myself walking slowly into my church to play drums. Running on about 3 hours sleep, and carrying an excruciatingly painful hangover for what must have been the sixth service in a row. My prayer in those situations was always "just help me get through this service…". That became a phrase that was being prayed far too often, and yet God graciously accepted it time after time. On one particular Sunday after praying "just help me get through this service", God responded clear as day with *"So is that how much I'm worth then? And is that how much you value a gift I have given you?"*.

It hit me like a train and I was immediately reminded of Cain and Abel's story. Specifically how Cain gave the absolute MINIMUM that was required just to get by, and God rejected it as if he would rather Cain hadn't bothered. Giving the minimum requirement had become my normality, and just trooping through a service was deemed an acceptable code of conduct. Those two questions from God brought about some serious questions about my lifestyle choices and general faith. At that moment, the concept of 'giving our best' was put onto paper and I felt it was something that needed to be shared somehow.

As with so many situations in life, God makes ALL things work for his good. Although that was a tough morning, in a way it brought about the basis of this book. The whole attitude that was explored in Chapter 2 surrounding "giving our best" is what can shape us as players, as disciples, and as Christ-centred characters. It is a life-changing concept that even effects how we operate on a daily basis. It is so important to never forget the difference between Cain and Abel's offerings.

It's important to remember that God's discipline and God's love can sometimes look exactly the same. And that in order to live within a worship-filled life, everything we do requires the absolute best that we can give.

This follows nicely onto the next question and paragraph. How does this idea look within a worship/drumming context?

WORSHIPPING THROUGH OUR INSTRUMENT

It's a funny concept when you think about it; worshipping through hitting something with a stick. But it is exactly that. If I'm going to worship by hitting something with a stick, then I am going to MEAN every single hit. This doesn't mean volume, strength or force; this is more about intention, awareness, and mindset. It is possible to really speak through this instrument and it carries real power and potential for moving people.

There are countless situations where a worship leader has dropped out all other instruments and just let the drums thunder on, and it is something that really resonates and speaks to people. Communicating through our instrument is a joy and something that we can spend our whole lives learning. Playing prophetically to aid a congregation in how they meet with their Father is a truly amazing feeling. The starting point for this is simply one big question, a question to always be asking when we are playing; 'WHY DO I WANT TO PLAY THIS?'.

There is a very fine line between 'using your skill' and 'showing off'. A very fine line that only you can really call. A tricky thing to judge as drummers is whether we are playing something to showcase our skill or to glorify God. It is a concept that requires regular thought and is something to keep re-checking ourselves on. If you are a Drummer that is practicing and working on your craft, you are going to be developing yourself as a musician and pushing your ideas and skill. This is great and super beneficial, but the struggle comes when you realise that you now have potential to really 'over-play' if you wanted to. As soon as you realise your pool of creative ideas is pretty deep, that is the moment that you need to be spiritually intentional about what you are playing.

This comes down to one thing; HUMILITY. Humbleness is preached about a lot in churches and is so applicable to musicians. When we have spent years crafting ourselves as drummers, that is when this point becomes crucial and also beneficial for how we worship through our instrument. The book of James sums it up perfectly; *Humble yourselves before the Lord, and he will lift you up* (James 4:10). Being humble in our musicianship is one of the ways we worship while playing. Just because we can throw in our super-chops doesn't mean we should. There is something so special about a drummer with all the skill in the world, who is choosing to keep the beat simple and solid, so that the rest of the band and congregation are comfortable and are able to worship.

Although, sometimes something flashier and skilful is actually needed! This can then get really awkward when thinking, "Am I doing this for me or for the Kingdom". It's a tricky one. My advice for this is not to think too much. Something that I have found really useful is to be continually praying while I'm drumming. I really believe that God communicates with his musicians and can sometimes actually give the green light for us to really give it some, but only when he needs us to. Drums are powerful, that message has been expressed throughout this whole book, so sometimes it is good to use that power to help people reach another spiritual revelation.

There have been only a handful of musical experiences where I have actually been left tear-filled and emotionally overwhelmed, and they have all involved knowing that my drumming was used to help people worship. When Jesus said, *"if they were to keep quiet, then the stones would cry out"* he gave a beautiful picture of this worshipful expression. If our voices aren't a way of expressing our worship, then our drums are the next go-to tool. Express your worship through your drumming. When musicians are worshipping through their instruments, giving it all back to God and not thinking about themselves or their playing, it genuinely feels like they touch on a different sound altogether. It is a feeling that is indescribable, something that I started to live for and something that felt was so much bigger than myself. Always be humble, always be intentional about what you are playing, and always be seeking God's will first in everything we do (including our drumming).

WORSHIPPING THROUGH OUR CHARACTER, AS WELL AS OUR MUSICIANSHIP

This point has the potential to turn into a whole other book and there are thousands of people far more qualified than myself to speak on this. This paragraph is going to zero in on one idea; being worshipful when we drum needs to also transcend into our characters as people. It is one thing to be a worshipful, spirit-filled musician, but if that does not reflect or appear within our day to day living then it is fruitless.

"This is how my Father is glorified, when you produce a lot of fruit and so prove to be my disciples" (John 15:8). To put it simply; **We are disciples first, drummers second.**

Our walk with God should always come first, always. As someone who is extremely career minded and goal oriented, it can be a daily reminder and struggle to put Christ before everything. There is no doubt that at one point my career became an obsession and an idol. Gaining recognition and success as a drummer took priority over God and there has been some humbling, yet invaluable lessons that were a reminder to put him first again. *"Draw near to God, and he will draw near to you..."* (James 4:8) couldn't be a truer statement.

When our validation and self-worth are subject to our drumming achievements, we put ourselves in a position to really damage ourselves. There is no denying that it would be an amazing accomplishment to make the front cover of a Drum Magazine, but my validation and self-worth should not be reliant on that happening. It is a challenge, but is also healthy to hold our drumming where it belongs; in HIS hands to be used how HE wants.

FINAL THOUGHTS

A final thought; Church family is so important for keeping ourselves in check. I am so blessed with the musicians and non-musicians that I have around me. They celebrate in my successes but also remind me where my priorities should be. They push me forward and encourage me to go after life and opportunities, but they are also there to comfort when disappointment comes. When Community is done properly it is invaluable in maintaining a healthy spiritual walk. Having been in both healthy and unhealthy community environments, I can safely say the two are not even remotely alike. *"As iron sharpens iron, so one person sharpens another."* (Proverbs 27:17). Your community as a worship team and with the rest of your church can be so beneficial and important. Support each other, pray together, socialise with one another, encourage each other, and be involved in each other's lives.

If I had to give a final word for this book that has taken me years to put into practice and can redefine how we view ourselves, our God, and our playing, it would be this:

WE ARE DISCIPLES FIRST, DRUMMERS SECOND.
First and foremost we are called to be his children, and how we use our drumming is a byproduct of that initial calling.
Thank you for reading, and God bless!

"A FIELD MANUAL;
BECAUSE IT NEEDS TO BE TAKEN INTO THE FIELD"